WASPS

WASPS

A Drawing Room Comedy
For Distempered Times

Sally Clark

Talonbooks
1998

Talonbooks
#104—3100 Production Way
Burnaby, British Columbia, Canada V5A 4R4

Typeset in New Baskerville and Frutiger and printed and bound in
Canada by Hignell Printing.

First Printing: October 1998

Talonbooks are distributed in Canada by General Distribution Services,
325 Humber College Blvd., Toronto, Ontario, Canada M9W 7C3;
Tel.:(416) 213-1919; Fax:(416) 213-1917.

Talonbooks are distributed in the U.S.A. by General Distribution
Services Inc., 85 Rock River Drive, Suite 202, Buffalo, New York, U.S.A.
14207-2170; Tel.:1-800-805-1083; Fax:1-800-481-6207.

Canadian Cataloguing in Publication Data

Clark, Sally, 1953-
  Wasps

  A play.
  ISBN 0-88922-398-X

  I. Title.
  PS8555.L37197W37 1998   C812'.54   C98-910732-9
  PR9199.3.C5235W37 1998

WASPS was first produced by Air-Conditioned Theatre at the Factory Theatre Studio Cafe in Toronto, Ontario from March 24 to April 14, 1996 with the following cast:

VAL	Arlene Mazerolle
CYRIL	Allan Morgan
SONDRA/SAM	Beverley Cooper
ANDREW BLETT	Stuart Clow
MARGE TURNBULL	Nancy MacLeod
MISS PEARCE	Clare Coulter

Director	Derek Boyes
Producer	Ken Burns
Stage Manager	Diane Konkin
Set & Costume Design	Andrew Burke-Hall
Lighting	Ken Burns

Assist. Stage Manager	Ken Benoy
Studio technician	Jonathan Rooke
Wardrobe/Co-ordinator/Props	Shawna Harvey
with assistance from	Kyle Glencross
	Elizabeth McCallum

Wigs	Theatrix
Head Carpenter	Doug Morum

WASPS was produced by Origins Theatre Projects at the Vancouver Little Theatre in Vancouver, B.C. from October 9 to October 18, 1997 with the following cast:

VAL	Jillian Fargey
CYRIL	Mark Weatherley
SONDRA/SAM	Peg Christopherson
ANDREW BLETT	Steven Campbell-Hill
MARGE TURNBULL, XEROX WOMAN, OPRAH	Lesley Ewen
MISS PEARCE, WOMAN A, EVELYN SNARPLES, JEAN & UNCLE CALVIN	Christine Willes
LIBRARY KIDS	Michael Trafananko
	Alia Ozdenir

Director	Sally Clark
Producer	Donnard MacKenzie
Sets & Lighting Design	Yvan Morissette
Costume Design	Tyler Tone
Sound Design	Sally Clark
Stage Manager/Sound Operator	Sharon Thompson
Associate Producer	Jim Schiebler

ACKNOWLEDGEMENTS

Arlene Mazarolle and Derek Boyes asked me if I had a play that would be suitable for their company, Air-Conditioned Theatre. I had just started *WASPS*. It was wonderful to write and know that someone was anxiously awaiting the final draft. I'd like to thank Arlene, Derek and Nancy MacLeod for their support and encouragement.

I would also like to thank Robin Fulford, Platform Nine Theatre, Norma Jenckes, the Ontario Arts Council and the Laidlaw Foundation for their generosity and support.

CHARACTERS

VAL, a librarian, aged in her thirties
CYRIL, her husband, a professor, aged in his thirties
SONDRA, a travel agent, aged in her thirties
MISS PEARCE, a librarian, aged fifty
ANDREW BLETT, aged in his thirties
MARGE TURNBULL, a book collector, aged in her thirties

WOMAN A
XEROX WOMAN
CHILD
ANOTHER CHILD
MRS. FARNSWORTH, a library patron, aged seventy
EVELYN SNARPLES, a neighbour
UNCLE CALVIN

TV: JEAN
       OPRAH

This play can be performed by 6 actors: 4 women and 2 men.

If you are a collective or an amateur group and it doesn't matter if people get paid, then cast it with as many people as you like.

The play should move quickly, like a farce. The running time should be 45 minutes for each act.

ACT ONE

Scene 1

*Buzzing sound of a swarm of angry wasps. The buzzing
gets louder, changing from wasps to the sound of an
electric razor. A worried, frightened-looking man with a
half-shaved head runs for his life, hotly pursued by a
woman with a shaved head, a buzzing razor held aloft
and a very intent look on her face.*

Blackout. mood ⇒ off the wall , not part of
disjointed   narrative

Scene 2

VAL's apartment. VAL is on the phone. CYRIL stands behind her. He nuzzles her neck.

VAL: Hi. Guess what, Mum! I'm married!! Isn't that exciting! *(slight pause)* Well, I think it's exciting. His name's Cyril. Cyril Winton-Smythe. Of course, he's nice. Now, don't get upset. It was just too exciting! He swept me off my feet. I'm in love, I'm in love, I'm in love! Don't cry, Mum. Bye. Say hi to Dad. *(hangs up)*

CYRIL: Do you think you should have hung up like that?

VAL: It was the answering machine.

CYRIL: Oh.

VAL: Okay. Your turn.

CYRIL: I don't know where they are.

VAL: Really? They're on vacation?

CYRIL: Sort of. One day—they just suddenly decided that they didn't want to be parents anymore, so they took off.

VAL: My friend's parents are doing that, too. You turn thirty, want to buy a house and suddenly your parents are living in Florida and not returning your calls.

CYRIL: I was fourteen.

VAL: What?

CYRIL: Yes. They had already put me in an English boarding school so I guess it didn't really matter. In terms of my life, they were already gone.

VAL: That's awful. You were abandoned.

CYRIL: Yes. I was, I guess. They might be in England. They liked England.

VAL: What did you do when it happened?

CYRIL: Um—this is a little embarrassing.

VAL: What?

CYRIL: I don't know how to say this—well—ah—I—ah— was a child prodigy.

VAL: You were?

CYRIL: Yes. I was a genius.

VAL: Really? You wouldn't know it.

CYRIL: Anyway, I got very upset and discovered a math theorem. Several, in fact. I was world famous for a couple of years. Well—you know, that sort of stuff.

VAL: No, I don't, actually. World famous?

CYRIL: In math circles, yes. I was given my doctorate. Actually, a few doctorates. I was at Oxford. Youngest professor there. Taught there for a few years. Then I came back to Canada. *→ geographical location*

VAL: Why'd you do that?

CYRIL: I was born here. Besides, I have family here.

VAL: What a weird thing for parents to do. You're so stoic about it.

CYRIL: Oh well, these things happen.

VAL: You poor baby. *(starts to kiss him)*

CYRIL: They did reappear a few years ago for our family reunion.

VAL: Oh. Well. That's nice, I guess.

CYRIL: Yeah. They stuck around for a while. Then they took off again. *(slight pause)* Darling....

VAL: I love it when you call me "darling." It's so English.

CYRIL: Darling, do you think you should have married me?

VAL: Of course! I love you. What a strange question.

CYRIL: We don't know each other.

VAL: Cyril, we're madly in love.

CYRIL: Yes. I know we're madly in love but we don't know each other. I have quirks.

VAL: Marriage is discovery. We'll get to know each other. What sort of quirks?

CYRIL: *(looks around)* I like your apartment.

VAL: Our apartment now!

CYRIL: Yes. It's nice. Homey.

VAL: You know, we should have rented a suite tonight.

CYRIL: Oh God! I'm sorry.

VAL: I've made our own little bridal suite. Take me! *(leaps into his arms)*

> *CYRIL, with VAL in his arms, staggers to the threshold of their bedroom. He stops at the threshold.*

CYRIL: Oh. *(starts to put VAL down)*

VAL: Don't put me down here! It's unlucky!

CYRIL: *(takes two steps away from the threshold, puts VAL down)* It's—ah—it's—ah—lovely. Rose petals. A tree.

VAL: A bower. That's a bower.

CYRIL: It's quite something. And pink. Everything is very pink in there.

VAL: What's wrong?

CYRIL: It's—ah—that suddenly I feel this enormous pressure to perform.

VAL: But we've made love ever since we met.

CYRIL: That's why I knew it was right. My sex drive was phenomenal.

VAL: Oh.

CYRIL: Didn't you think it was phenomenal?

VAL: No. I thought it was normal. Don't worry, Cyril. *(tries to drag him in)*

CYRIL: No—really. I can't go in there.

VAL: Later?

CYRIL: Maybe. *(stands and peers in)*

VAL: I'll take out the bower.

CYRIL: I need time to adjust to the crisis.

VAL: It's just a pink room.

CYRIL: No. The marriage. On the psychological level, falling in love, marriage, death, destruction of property by flood or fire—are all the same. They're all upsetting events to the psyche. *(pulls out paper and pencil, sits down and starts working)*

VAL: What are you doing?

CYRIL: Sssh! *(writes)* Mmm. Yes. Uh huh.

VAL: Cyril?

CYRIL: When I'm in crisis mode, I get very creative.

VAL: *(puzzled)* Oh. That's nice.

    CYRIL continues writing.

VAL: Will you be long?

CYRIL: Huh? Sorry. Yes, all night, I think.

VAL: Oh.

CYRIL: *(walks over to VAL, he's still scribbling stuff down)*
Night, darling. *(kisses her, walks back to couch, still
scribbling)*

⌊ VAL: Is this one of your quirks? ⌟

↳ foreshadowing ⌋

- @ this pt, conflict has not yet soared,
   mood / atmosphere - absurd.

Scene 3

Travel agent on the phone.

SONDRA: Gulliver's Travels. Why hello, Caroline. No, no, I
    haven't forgotten you but all the flights to Helsinki are
    booked up that day. I know it's strange and who would
    want to go to Helsinki in February but apparently
    everyone does and they're all leaving on the day you've
    requested. Now you can arrive four days before or four
    days after but you can't arrive on that day. You simply
    can't do it. *(stifles a laugh)* Pardon? No. That was a
    cough. So, you'll take the one four days before? Good.
    (hangs up and laughs)

Scene 4 *⌐Short scenes- quick tempo* *quick myth* *→in keeping with farce style*

Front desk at a very busy library. There is a line-up of people waiting to sign books out. VAL is alone at the desk and trying to do it as quickly as possible. A phone is ringing. VAL ignores it and tries to sign out books. A woman who doesn't speak English struggles with the nearby Xerox machine. She deposits money. It doesn't work She kicks the machine. She waits. Nothing happens.

WOMAN A: I'd like to order *Body Building for Women* by Trixie Hyman.

VAL nods and hurriedly writes it down on a slip of paper.

ANDREW BLETT: Are the computers down?

VAL: Yes.

ANDREW: They're down a lot here.

VAL: Yes. All the time.

WOMAN A: That's H-Y-M-A-N. And *Muscles! Yours to Develop!* by Babs Schumaker. And *The Way of All Flesh* by Samuel Butler.

VAL: One of these books is going to be a profound disappointment.

WOMAN A: Huh?

VAL: They should be here in three to four weeks.

WOMAN A nods and moves on. VAL checks out the books of ANDREW BLETT.

ANDREW: Well, I guess there're some advantages to the computers being down all the time.

VAL: Pardon?

ANDREW: You're not as likely to get carpel tunnel syndrome. A lot of librarians get that now, don't they?

VAL: Yes. They do.

ANDREW: So. You won't get that. *(brightly, warming to the topic)* And your unborn foetus will be safe, too.

VAL: My what?

ANDREW: Oh. Sorry. *(grabs books and rushes out)*

A small BOY approaches the desk.

BOY: Gimme a book on Labour Day.

VAL: Please.

BOY: Huh?

VAL: Gimme a book on Labour Day, please.

BOY: You want one, too?

VAL: A whole book. Just on Labour Day.

BOY nods

VAL: Is this for Mrs. Wannamaker's class?

BOY nods.

VAL: What is it with her? Every year, twenty of you guys
come in and want a book on Labour day. It's a holiday.
That's all. The first Monday in September. A holiday to
celebrate Labour. There's no book about Labour Day.
It's a day. That's all. One day.

BOY: *(mumbles)* I need pictures.

VAL: Are you the one who's cutting the pictures out of our
books?!

XEROX WOMAN: *(to VAL)* EY!

*The XEROX WOMAN, having launched into a full frontal
attack on the machine, decides now to ask for VAL's help.
She stands and snaps her fingers at VAL. While VAL is
momentarily distracted by the XEROX WOMAN, the BOY
flees.*

VAL: *(pleasantly to XEROX WOMAN)* May I help you?

XEROX WOMAN: EY! EY!

VAL: Madame, I am not a cab. If you'd like to come over
here and tell me what the problem is, I'd be happy to
help you.

*The XEROX WOMAN is totally baffled by VAL's speech.
She kicks the machine.*

VAL: Please, don't kick the Xerox machine.

XEROX WOMAN kicks it again

VAL: You don't need to kick the machine. Maybe it's out of paper. I'll just look and see.

>   *XEROX WOMAN kicks it again*

VAL: DON'T KICK THE MACHINE!!! *(chases XEROX WOMAN away from the Xerox machine)*

>   *MISS PEARCE, the Branch Librarian enters.*

MISS PEARCE: Miss McIntosh.

VAL: *(stops in her tracks) (the XEROX WOMAN has fled)* Yes, Miss Pearce.

MISS PEARCE: You were chasing that woman around the library.

VAL: But she comes in every day and kicks the Xerox machine. Every day!

MISS PEARCE: She's one of our multicultural patrons. We mustn't be nasty to the ethnic minorities. You must control yourself, Miss McIntosh.

VAL: What about that bag lady? She kicked the machine and you chased her?

MISS PEARCE: Bag ladies are still fair game. *(pulls out air freshener)* Where is she?

VAL: Miss Pearce?

MISS PEARCE: Yes.

VAL: It's Mrs. Winton-Smythe.

MISS PEARCE: That's her name? The bag lady?

VAL: No. Me. I got married a few days ago.

MISS PEARCE: Married?! You're kidding.

VAL: No.

MISS PEARCE: I guess you never thought you'd get
     married.

VAL: Why not?

MISS PEARCE: Well, you know. The lifestyle.

VAL: Librarian, you mean. Miss Pearce, you mustn't buy
     into that myth about librarians. That we're all a bunch
     of spinsters who wear oversize glasses, big tweed skirts
     and sensible shoes.

> *VAL and MISS PEARCE suddenly look at their clothes.*
> *They are wearing glasses, tweed skirts and sensible shoes.*

VAL: Well, I've broken out, Miss Pearce.

MISS PEARCE: Did you go somewhere nice on your
     honeymoon?

VAL: Ah—we're still deciding.

MISS PEARCE: Oh. Well, congratulations!

VAL: Thanks. Can I take a long lunch hour today?

MISS PEARCE: Since it's your honeymoon, of course.

Scene 5

Travel agency.

VAL: Hello, my name is Mrs. Winton-Smythe. I'd like to
look at your honeymoon packages.

SONDRA: Mrs. Winton-Smythe.

VAL: Yeah. I just had to say it out loud. You know. See how
it sounded. *(points to brochure)* This one looks
interesting.

SONDRA: As in "Cyril" Winton-Smythe?

VAL: Well yes. He's a client of yours.

SONDRA: Is that what he told you?

VAL: I assume he's a client. I found your card—

SONDRA: Where?

VAL: Pardon?

SONDRA: Where did you find the card?

VAL: I don't know. On his desk. My travel agent committed
suicide last week so I thought I'd try you. It's supposed
to be a surprise. Cyril doesn't know about the
honeymoon.

SONDRA: Does he know about the marriage?

VAL: What sort of question is that!

SONDRA: Sorry. I guess you'd like a short-term package. A day or two max.

VAL: No. Not necessarily. I was thinking of three weeks in Acapulco.

SONDRA: Three weeks? *(meaningfully)* You think he can manage that?

VAL: WHO ARE YOU?

SONDRA: Sondra Elworthy. It says so on my card. It's a tough business. Who was your agent?

VAL: Lynn Dormack. Best Deal Travels.

SONDRA: *(hears "Bestial")* It's awful when they get into Devil worshipping. But I don't know. It's the life, I guess. Booking. Rebooking. Cancellation insurance. Cheap charters. You just crack.

VAL: BEST DEAL.

SONDRA: Oh yes, I see. How long had you known her?

VAL: Look, this really doesn't have anything to do with—

SONDRA: Don't you care? She worked very hard on your behalf. Aren't you in the least upset?

VAL: Yes. It was too bad.

SONDRA: So, how long had you known her?

VAL: Ten years.

SONDRA: Ten years! Well, I hope you went to her funeral.

VAL: No, I didn't! And I'm not going to yours, either!!
  (pause) You're not his travel agent, are you!

SONDRA: Yes, I am.

VAL: No you're not!

SONDRA: Am too!

VAL: Are not!

SONDRA: All right, I'm not. I'm his lover.

VAL: AAAAAGH!

SONDRA: See. I knew it would upset you. When did you
  get married?

VAL: Three days ago.

SONDRA: *(looks at calendar)* Tuesday. Yes. He said he was
  busy then.

VAl: Busy?! Busy!? We were getting married!!

SONDRA: How was the honeymoon? *(laughs)*

VAL: How long have you and Cyril been—

SONDRA: Oh. Five years, I guess. Don't worry about
  it. The man has no sex drive. Being his lover is a
  non-event. The thing I find so fascinating is that Cyril
  goes to such lengths to introduce us. All the members
  of his harem.

VAL: Harem?

SONDRA: I'm supposed to be jealous of you because you are now the lucky recipient of his sexual advances. I mean, really! He gets it up about once a month and bingo, it's gone.

VAL: Well, I wouldn't say that.

SONDRA: Don't play the "I'm the one who brings out the hidden passion" game. He's terrible and you know it.

VAL: He's very good. Very exciting.

SONDRA: I suppose I can't blame you. I said the exact same thing to Denise. Has he put you "on hold" yet?

VAL: Who's Denise?

SONDRA: One of his exes. She used to sing "Mean to Me."

VAL: Mean to me?

SONDRA: *(sings)* "Mean to me, why are you always so mean to me?..."

VAL: *(looks around)* Is your office always so unattended?

SONDRA: I turned the phones off. He was mean to her. He was mean to me, too but I'd never sing that song. I mean, I couldn't. It was Denise's. Caroline used to sing "Lemon Tree." *(sings)* "Lemon tree, very pretty...."

VAL: Caroline. Right. *(stands up)* Well that's enough. I won't be booking my HONEYMOON—my TWO MONTHS IN ACAPULCO here with you. And Cyril's appointments are now ended. Do I make myself clear? OVER. KAPUT. FINIS!

SONDRA: You're perfect. You're exactly right.

VAL: Don't try that masochistic approach with me.

SONDRA: Features. Build. Everything's there. Hair's not quite right. Lose some weight, change the clothes and you're perfect. You're so close. You're almost there. Are you an artist as well? Cyril's sister is an artist.

VAL: He has a sister?

SONDRA: Yes. Didn't he tell you?

VAL: Um—yes—it slipped my mind.

SONDRA: Two sisters. Andrea, the dental hygienist. That's the "sister" sister.

VAL: The "sister" sister?

SONDRA: And Sam.

VAL: He has a brother who's pretending to be a sister?

SONDRA: Samantha. She lives in Winnipeg.

VAL: Really. How pleasant. Well, I'll certainly be delighted to meet her. Someone who isn't an ex-lover. Someone who doesn't SING! *(storms out)*

> SONDRA *flicks a switch. The phones start ringing madly.*

Scene 6

Home. VAL walks in. CYRIL rushes up to her.

CYRIL: Hello darling. I haven't had such a surge of creativity since my parents disappeared. I love being married! *(hugs her)*

VAL: I met your lover, today.

CYRIL: My lover.

VAL: Sondra.

CYRIL: *(blank)* Sondra.

VAL: Do you have another one?

CYRIL: Another what?

VAL: Lover.

CYRIL: I don't know what you're talking about.

VAL: Sondra claimed that she was your lover and that there was a whole slew of them out there.

CYRIL: Out where?

VAL: Out where lovers are. Don't be so obtuse.

CYRIL: Where are lovers? Whatever happened to love, anyway?

VAL: Don't change the subject.

CYRIL: I've almost got this theorem nailed down. Can we get back to this another time?

VAL: NO!

CYRIL: It's complicated—

VAL: She's your lover.

CYRIL: No, she's not! She's my—ah—she's my...Stalker.

VAL: Your what?!

CYRIL: My Stalker. She's been stalking me for years. At first, I tried to get away but that only made it worse. So, I learned to live with it. Take her out for lunch. Keep in touch.

VAL: How much in touch?

CYRIL: Really darling. You mustn't believe her. She's delusional.

VAL: What about Caroline? Denise?

CYRIL: They're just old girlfriends. Sondra stalked them too.

VAL: Why didn't you tell me about her?

CYRIL: Well, she's a troublemaker, isn't she. Look how upset she's made you. Over nothing! You're sweet when you get jealous. *(hugs VAL)*

VAL: She said you had sisters.

CYRIL: Yes.

VAL: I didn't know that.

CYRIL: Oh. Well, I have two sisters. You don't mind, do you?

VAL: Of course not. It's just that you never mentioned them. I'm sorry, Cyril. I'm feeling a bit insecure these days.

CYRIL: Why?

VAL: It's your quirk. I feel unattractive.

CYRIL: I'm sorry, Val. I can't help it. Anyway, you can't force desire.

VAL: You don't desire me?

CYRIL: Oh. I shouldn't have said that. No, no, of course, I desire you. Just not now. Sometime, I'm sure it will all come flooding back. Maybe if you cut your hair. Really short.

VAL: Short?

CYRIL: You'd look sexy with short hair. And dye it blonde! Lemon blonde!

VAL: Fake blonde.

CYRIL: Well, it's just an idea. *(plays with her hair)* It's just that with your hair like that, you look a bit like my mother.

Scene 7

Travel agency. SONDRA is on the phone.

SONDRA: Hello Denise, I'm so glad I reached you. Koala's
full. So, here's what I have. It's a charter. Air Platypus.
No. No flyer points. You fly from Toronto to Chicago.
Wait three hours. Chicago to Los Angeles. I had a hard
time getting you that one. You stay overnight in Los
Angeles—oh—you'll have to pay for that—catch the 4
a.m. flight from Los Angeles to Honolulu. Wait till
Thursday. Yes, I know but Air Platypus only flies on
Thursdays. Well, Thursday's not that far away. And
you're staying in the Journey's End Motel, with a
spectacular view of the volcano. No, you're not that
close to it. Pardon? Yes, I'm sure it's inactive. Anyway,
it's only for a couple of days so what the hell. Catch the
2:00 a.m. flight from Honolulu on Thursday and land
in Auckland. Yes. I know you wanted to go to Australia
but New Zealand's close. So, you'll take it? Good.
(laughs)

Scene 8

The library. VAL now has short cropped dyed blonde hair. A small CHILD whispers something to her. VAL leans down in a threatening manner. The XEROX WOMAN is at the Xerox machine. She puts her money in. It falls through.

VAL: This is for Mrs. Wannamaker's class, isn't it?

CHILD nods.

VAL: How does she do it? How does she think of these. Subjects so big they're impossible to describe and yet, so small, there's no book.

CHILD: Mrs. Wannamaker says there is a book here on Remembrance Day.

VAL: Yes. There was. THERE WAS. Until you guys came along and cut out all the pictures so there's no book anymore. Remember *B.C. Yours to Enjoy!?* Well, nobody's enjoying it now. Does Mrs. Wannamaker ask you to cut out the pictures? Does she?

CHILD: Where's the book?

VAL: We don't have it. It's gone. You've just got me. *(announces)* REMEMBRANCE DAY. The first Remembrance Day was November the 11th, 1918. It marked the end of the First World War. So you could read all about the First World War and then you'd know what you're supposed to remember. Or if the First World War doesn't appeal to you, you could read about World War II, Or Korea. Or Vietnam. Any war will do.

MISS PEARCE crosses over to her office. She gives VAL a pointed look.

VAL: Then there's the Remembrance Day poem. "IN FLANDERS FIELDS, THE POPPIES BLOW BETWEEN THE CROSSES ROW ON ROW...." You say that poem and then you shut up for two minutes and you remember the dead. And you have to do it from 11:00 a.m. to 11:02 a.m. every November 11th. And then, so you'll know when to stop remembering, some bugler plays "Day is Done." *(hums it)* Dah dah dah, dah dah dah.... And then they fire off a cannon and you go home.

CHILD: Can I remember my Aunt Ethel?

VAL: Did your Aunt Ethel fight in a war?

CHILD: No.

VAL: WELL THEN YOU CAN'T REMEMBER HER! You can only remember the people who died in a war. And if you spend those two minutes thinking of someone else, the Remembrance Day police will come and beat you up!

CHILD: Oh. *(walks away, very disturbed)*

The XEROX WOMAN starts to get angry with the machine. VAL is about to help her when SONDRA appears.

SONDRA: Hi.

VAL: Oh God, you! *(VAL tries to leave the desk)*

XEROX WOMAN: EY! EY!
(stands and snaps her fingers at VAL)

VAL: I should help this woman—

SONDRA: Look—I-ah—I'd like to apologize for the things
I said to you—making you think Cyril and I were
lovers—I mean, we were lovers but not lately—though
from time to time—

People in the library listen. VAL notices.

VAL: We're in a library.

SONDRA: *(looks around)* Oh. Sorry. *(loud whisper)* We used
to make love a lot and he was really good.

VAL: Yes—you've already filled me in on that episode of
your life.

SONDRA: *(normal voice)* Oh—well, you see, that part's true.
But not everything I say is true. Part of my illness. I'm a
confabulist.

The XEROX WOMAN starts hitting the machine.

VAL: A what?

SONDRA: A confabulist. We embellish events. My doctor
says it's because of memory loss. I don't remember the
true event so I make something up.

VAL: You mean you're a liar?

SONDRA: That is a derogatory term and one which the
confabulists are seeking to eliminate.

VAL: But that's what you do. You tell lies.

The XEROX WOMAN starts kicking the machine.

33

SONDRA: No. I CONFABULATE! You're a Neo-rightist Wasp bigot, aren't you?

VAL: I'm a what?

SONDRA: I bet you call little people midgets.

VAL: Only if they ARE midgets. Otherwise I call them DWARVES.

SONDRA: BIGOT!

VAL: LIAR!

XEROX WOMAN is rigorously kicking the machine.

VAL: STOP KICKING THE XEROX MACHINE!

XEROX WOMAN glares at VAL and kicks it again.

SONDRA: *(to XEROX WOMAN)* GO ON! BEAT IT! GET OUDDA HERE!!

SONDRA chases the XEROX WOMAN out of the library. VAL looks around guiltily.

SONDRA: *(returns)* Look, I only came 'cause Cyril begged me to. Said you were so neurotic and insecure, you were driving him crazy. I'm trying to fix things up.

VAL: You're doing a wonderful job. Fine.

SONDRA: And you better get over your prejudice 'cause that's how Cyril and I met. Confabulists Anonymous.

VAL: Cyril is not a liar.

SONDRA: Actually it started off as a coke rehab centre. The shrink who ran it saw that what we really had in common was confabulation so he started another clinic.

VAL: Cyril has never lied to me.

SONDRA: He leaves things out, though, doesn't he. Little things like me, Caroline, Denise, Rudolfo—

VAL: It was unimportant.

SONDRA: Bury the past, eh.

VAL: Yes.

SONDRA: Why did you chop your hair off and bleach it?

VAL: A change.

SONDRA: Cyril asked you to, didn't he?

VAL: So what if he did?

SONDRA: Nothing. *(laughs)* Almost forgot. Your honeymoon package. I've been looking into it.

VAL: No—please—don't bother.

SONDRA: Don't you want a honeymoon?

VAL: NO!

   ANDREW BLETT appears at the desk.

SONDRA: Hair didn't help, eh? Didn't do it for him? *(shrugs)* Used to work. *(leaves)*

ANDREW: Hi. *(looks meaningfully at VAL)*

VAL: Oh. Hi. You're in here quite often.

ANDREW: *(embarrassed)* Yes. I hope that's all right.

VAL: Oh. Sorry. Of course, it's all right. Did you want to ask me something?

ANDREW: Is the computer still down?

VAL: Yes. I'm afraid so.

ANDREW: Oh! *(pause, as though restraining himself from an indecent act) (suddenly bursts out)* I'd like the entire collected works of Pushkin, Tolstoy, Dostoevsky and Solzhenitsyn, please!

VAL: Pardon?

ANDREW: *(embarrassed)* I guess that is a bit excessive. I've looked on your shelves and I can't find any of these books.

VAL: Someone stole all our Russian novels.

ANDREW: *(righteously indignant)* That's awful! What sort of fiend would do that!

VAL: And the worst of it is, this person probably doesn't even read the books.

ANDREW: *(outraged)* No!

VAL: I'll order them in from another branch for you. I just need your card, please.

ANDREW: Oh. But the lines are down. What do you need my card for?

VAL: Name, address, have to write it down on the forms.

ANDREW: Andrew Blett. 1702 Brookfield Avenue.

VAL: I need your card.   -

ANDREW reluctantly hands her his library card. VAL looks through a small Rolodex file.

ANDREW: What are you doing?

VAL: This is just a formality. *(leafs through the file, looks at a card)* AHA! ANDREW BLETT!

ANDREW: *(nervously)* Yes?

VAL: YOU'RE NOTORIOUS!!

ANDREW: Well, I run a small theatre company but I wouldn't say—

VAL: *(runs around the desk, waving the library card)* A D.B.! A D.B.! THE TOP D.B. IN THE SYSTEM AND I GOT HIM!!

ANDREW: A D.B.?

VAL: DELINQUENT BORROWER! *(rips page out of Rolodex and waves it in ANDREW's face)* You have one thousand, five hundred ninety-two dollars and forty-four cents in T by B's!!!

ANDREW: T by B's? T by B's? What are—

VAL: *(hisses at ANDREW)* Taken by Borrower. BOOKS! Books that you have stolen since 1984!! Oh God, Oh God, I'm getting too excited! A D.B.! Oh God, I can't believe it!! I've caught a D.B. And not just any D.B. but ANDREW BLETT!! MISS PEARCE!

MISS PEARCE: *(pokes her head in from off side)* Did you say Andrew Blett? D.B. since 1984?

VAL rushes over to tell her.

VAL: YES! YES!

MISS PEARCE: My GOD! My GOD!!

ANDREW decides to make a break for it. VAL runs after him. He leaps off stage and dodges in and out of the audience, VAL in hot pursuit. He exits. VAL returns a few minutes later, sobbing with rage.

VAL: I had him. I almost had him.

MISS PEARCE: There there, dear. It happens to the best of us.

VAL: Why is life so hard?

MISS PEARCE: You seem to be a bit overwrought these days. I thought newlyweds were supposed to be happy.

VAL nods glumly.

MISS PEARCE: I don't know how to say this, Miss McIntosh—sorry, Mrs. Smith Wynne-Jones—

VAL: Winton-Smythe.

MISS PEARCE: Whatever. *(hauls VAL off to one side)* You seem to be getting a little aggressive with the patrons. You frightened three children yesterday.

VAL: Sorry.

MISS PEARCE: We are public servants here, Val. We are supposed to like the public. Granted, our particular public is composed of cheesy penny-pinching scumbags who are too cheap to even buy books. But we are supposed to like them. We are paid to like them. I don't think you like them very much, Val.

VAL: It's true, Miss Pearce. I don't.

MISS PEARCE: You need to release your antagonism. There's a job opening at Special Services. I suggest you apply for it.

VAL: I don't think a new job's going to help.

MISS PEARCE: Well then, let me put it another way. If you don't leave, I'm going to have to fire you.

VAL: Oh.

MISS PEARCE: Good. I'll set up an appointment for you tomorrow morning.

Scene 9

That night. CYRIL and VAL sit close together on the couch. CYRIL works on a math problem and strokes VAL's hair.

CYRIL: I like your hair this way.

VAL: You do.

CYRIL: Yeah. It suits you. *(kisses her neck)* But you know what would look great.

VAL: No?

CYRIL: A pair of those small wire-rimmed glasses.

VAL: Granny glasses. Then, I'd really look like a librarian.

CYRIL: Well, you'd have to change your image. Stop wearing those skirts and the flat-heeled shoes. Get rid of that cardigan.

VAL: But I love my cardigan.

CYRIL: It smells.

VAL: It's a nice smell. It smells of books.

CYRIL: *(sings)* "Marion, Madame Librarian."

VAL: All right, I'll ditch the cardigan.

CYRIL: Dress sleek.

VAL: Would you find me more attractive, then?

CYRIL: I always find you attractive.

VAL: You know what I mean.

CYRIL: Oh.

VAL: It's been two months.

CYRIL: Has it?

> *The phone rings. CYRIL leans over to answer it. He still has one arm around VAL.*

CYRIL: Hello. *(pause) (takes his arm away from VAL) (to VAL)* It's my sister, *(hushed pronouncement)* Sam.

CYRIL: *(intently listening)* Yes. Yes. All right. I will. How big? Of course, I will. When? Yes.

> *CYRIL hangs up the phone, puts on his coat and walks out the door.*

VAL: Where are you going?

CYRIL: I have to find Sam a house.

VAL: Now?

CYRIL: Yes. *(leaves)*

Scene 10

The next morning. Job interview. VAL and MARGE TURNBULL. MARGE wears a brown and orange Fortrel uniform.

MARGE: Main Office figures since I'm gonna be spending all day in the van with one of you guys, I should do the interviewing myself, like. Nice haircut.

VAL: Oh. Thanks.

MARGE: Trim. I like it trim.

VAL: I call it my Gertrude Stein look.

MARGE: *(brightens)* You like Gertrude Stein?

VAL: No! I mean, yes, I mean—she was a nice woman, I guess.

MARGE: Being a Book Collector ain't all easy street, ya know. Sometimes you gotta get tough with these dudes. I like the job you did on Blett. Real spunky.

VAL: He got away.

MARGE: Yeah but ya chased him down the street. If he hadn't taken a cab, ya would have nailed him. We'll find him.

VAL: Well, Miss Turnbull—

MARGE: Marge. Call me Marge. We're gonna be spending
a lot of time in that little van together. No sense being
formal now.

VAL: Um—what would I have to do exactly if I took this
job?

MARGE: Ya wouldn't have to bash any heads if that's what
yer thinking.

VAL: No—I wasn't think—

MARGE: Ya go to their door. ya knock on it real nice. They
answer and ya say, "May I come in?" and ya says this as
you're walking in the door and then ya might say—"I
am the Metropolitan Public Library Book Collector and
I have been authorized to confiscate property
belonging to the aforementioned." And of course,
you're running through their house looking for
contraband while ya say this. Then while they protest—
ya say AHA! and you start hauling their books off the
shelves. Worry about whether they're our books later.
Now if the guy's a problem, then ya say: "I hereby make
a Citizen's Arrest." This is a little personal innovation of
my own, like. I don't know whether you're allowed to
make a Citizen's Arrest or not but sounds good and
stops them in their tracks. Now I could probably handle
the job myself but I figured it might be nice to have
some company. A partner. Business partner, I mean.
The pay's fabulous and our time's our own. As long as
we bring in the quota, Main Office doesn't care what
we're up to. So, ya interested?

VAL: Well—

MARGE: Any questions?

VAL: Would I have to wear that uniform?

MARGE: Oh yeah, ya need the uniform. Otherwise you're just some schmoe. Ya wouldn't know it but I've worn this every day for three years. This stuff's amazing. You can pour anything on it. Just rolls right off. Doesn't need to be washed more than once a week. Nah, the uniform's best part of the job. I love a gal in a uniform. *(gives VAL a pointed look and laughs)*

   VAL laughs uncomfortably.

MARGE: Hey don't you worry. No sexual harassment on this job. No siree! Not like those big stud male librarians. I bet they're always coming onto ya.

VAL: Well—no, actually. Have you seen any big stud male librarians? I mean—there are a few male librarians but *(laughs)* I'm not their type.

MARGE: Yeah. I knew that.

VAL: No—no—I mean—the other way.

MARGE: *(confused)* Huh?

VAL: No—I mean, they're gay. I'm not gay.

MARGE: Look it's okay. You can level with me.

VAL: I'm not gay!

MARGE: Fine. You're not gay. So I guess you don't want the job 'cause I'm gay.

VAL: *(nervously)* Really?! I would never have—of course, that's not the reason—

MARGE: Yeah sure right, why else do ya think I'm in this fucking van! Isolate the queers! Fucking discrimination, that's what it is!!

VAL: What branch does this—ah—big stud male librarian work in?

Scene 11

MARGE and VAL. MARGE is knocking at a door, with Gestapo-like enthusiasm.

MARGE: WE KNOW YOU'RE IN THERE, MRS. FARNSWORTH. COME OUT WITH YOUR HANDS UP!!!

OLD WOMAN VOICE: YOU'LL NEVER GET ME ALIVE, COPPERS!

MARGE: Isn't she cute. Love those old wasps. *(yells)* I'M COMING IN, MRS. FARNSWORTH! WE'RE GONNA BUST DOWN THE DOOR!!

MRS. FARNSWORTH: No! Please! I just had it repainted!

MARGE: I'M COUNTING TO THREE, MRS. FARNSWORTH. ONE!

VAL: Marge, don't you think you're being a little harsh. You're terrorizing this poor old lady.

MARGE: Poor old lady, my ass. That old broad has Metro's entire collection of L.M. Montgomery. Everything. *Anne of Green Gables, Anne of Avonlea, Chronicles of Avonlea,* you name it. She got the hardcovers years ago but every goddamn paperback we buy, she snatches. TWO!

VAL: But maybe she loves those books. Maybe they remind her of her childhood. *(shouts)* IT'S OKAY, MRS. FARNSWORTH. IT'S OKAY TO LOVE *ANNE OF GREEN GABLES.* YOU MUSTN'T BE ASHAMED.

MRS. FARNSWORTH: Pardon?

VAL: *(shouts)* LET US IN. YOU DON'T NEED TO GIVE ALL THE BOOKS BACK. JUST THE PAPERBACKS.

MARGE: You're doing a deal with her?! Are you crazy! Those old wasps will take ya for everything ya got.

MRS. FARNSWORTH: *(pokes her head out of an upstairs window)* Did you say I love those books?! I want those books OUT! That smarmy simpering—And I've written to the CBC. I want that GODDAMN show off the air. That nauseating—National Treasure my eye! Those books are vile and should not be seen or read by anyone.

VAL: They offend you?!

MRS. FARNSWORTH: They're so sweet. They're so sickeningly sweet. Nobody used to notice before when I took them. That's 'cause people knew they were a pile of crap. But now? People think they're good. I'm burning every one. It's my duty as a librarian!

MARGE: THREE! *(smashes herself against the door)*

MRS. FARNSWORTH: *(screams)* AAAAAAAGH!

VAL: Marge! She used to be a librarian. God! Farnsworth. She was Head Librarian at City Hall for thirty years.

MARGE: The operative word is "was."

MARGE hurls herself against the door. The door opens. MRS. FARNSWORTH screams. MARGE goes hurtling through. VAL follows.

Scene 12

MARGE and VAL leave the scene of the crime.

MARGE: *(carrying boxes of books)* That was a huge haul.

VAL: It's awful what we did.

MARGE: A truly worthy opponent. I never thought of looking in the sock drawer. Nice work, Val.

VAL: I feel terrible.

MARGE: You know when she was Branch Head, she wrote plot summaries of all the books. Stuck it on the inside. My favourite was Kerouac's. "Disaffected youths seek adventure and find drugs instead." Every book he wrote, that was the summary. "Five disaffected youths, four disaffected youths...."

VAL: Mrs. Farnsworth was whimpering when we left.

MARGE: *(nods)* Mmmmhmmm.

VAL: And you don't feel badly about that.

MARGE: Nope.

VAL: Why not.

MARGE: Because she cares and we care. And that's what it's all about. Caring.

VAL: You know, Marge, I don't really feel that I belong in this job.

MARGE: You'll get onto it. Anyway, it's not like you have a choice. Whadja do to get put in The Van? Musta been somethin' awful.

VAL: Oh. Well. I've been under a lot of stress lately. I just got married and well, you know...my—ah—my—ah— husband *(starts sobbing)* He won't make love to me!! *(bursts into tears)*

MARGE: Geez! Sorry I asked.

VAL has a loud teary outburst.

MARGE: Oh. Sympathy. I guess you want sympathy. Gee, that's terrible. Not having sex with your husband. Men usually like to have sex, too. Boy, that's awful. Do you think he's gay?

VAL: Of course not! Why would you say that?

MARGE: If he's not having sex with you, then he must be having sex with someone.

VAL: Men aren't simply machines programmed for sex. They have feelings too, you know. Apparently, he just doesn't feel like it. Hasn't felt like it for some time.

MARGE: I'd be suspicious. Men aren't like women. They aren't capable of being celibate.

VAL: Come off it, Marge. Men can so be celibate. Look at priests. Sorry—bad example. Sailors—months at sea— oh well, maybe not. It is a good marriage. It's a perfectly good marriage with just one little snag.

MARGE: Big snag.

VAL: It might just be a passing phase. Cyril assures me it is. In every other respect, he has all the makings of a great husband. He's romantic.

MARGE: Just lacks punch, that's all.

VAL: He's not a crazy artist. He's not a drug addict. He's not an alcoholic.

MARGE: Oh well, you were smart to get him before he was snapped up by some other desperate woman.

VAL: He's intelligent. Practical. I can trust him with my bank account. He's good-looking. A great dancer. I've never gone out with a man who could dance. He's bad in bed which doesn't make sense because everyone always told me that guys who were great dancers were great in bed.

MARGE: Wait a minute. He doesn't have sex with you but when he does, it's bad. Is that what you're saying?

VAL: Well—

MARGE: Ditch him. He's no good. Send him back.

VAL: But I love him.

MARGE: Get over it. This love shit. I've taken a vacation from my love life.

VAL: You have?

MARGE: Yup. I'm a celibate lesbian.

VAL: Isn't that a contradiction in terms? How can you be a non-practising member of a sexually-defined group?

MARGE: If priests can fuck little boys, I can be a celibate lesbian.

VAL: Right.

MARGE: So, I guess you're worried now that you're a lesbian.

VAL: What?

MARGE: Sexually frustrated. No action from the husband. I'm sure you must be thinking: "Christ, I've married this boring dork and now, even he's turned out to be a problem. I can't deal with men. I must be a lesbian."

VAL: I never thought that.

MARGE: I've met tons of you gals. All you straight women, haven't been laid in years, all wondering if you're lesbians. Not everyone can be a lesbian, you know.

VAL: I don't want to be a lesbian.

MARGE: Denial. It starts with denial.

VAL: I'M NOT A LESBIAN!

MARGE: The fact is no one's getting laid happily, anymore. It might seem like all us lesbians are out there having a whale of a time but it's not true. Free Love has turned to ratshit in the last ten years. The party's over. No free rides. Nope. Now, it's all angst and regret and trauma. And if it's not that, then it's some awful business transaction like you have with your husband.

VAL: Cyril and I are in love!

MARGE: Good for you. *(starts looking through her papers)*

VAL: No, really, we are. *(muses)* Everything was great until we got married. Cyril's a little spooked. That's all.

MARGE: Uh huh. *(still looking)*

VAL: Maybe Cyril is testing me. Maybe he's pretending not to be interested in sex.

MARGE: *(jabs her finger on a name on the list)* Ah! Now here's someone I've been wanting to nail for some time. A U. of T. professor.

VAL: Of course! He's a professor. Yes. He's giving me a test. He's testing my love. That's it. It's a test!

Scene 13

Bedroom. VAL is in bed. CYRIL is under the covers.

VAL: Yes! Yes! Oh! Finally! Yes!

The phone rings during VAL's exclamations. CYRIL's hand darts out from the covers and answers it. A puzzled and annoyed expression crosses VAL's face. CYRIL sits up, still under the covers. He nods his head.

CYRIL: Yes. Mmmmhmm. Yes. Great! See you!

CYRIL hangs up the phone and starts to get dressed.

CYRIL: Sam's coming over.

VAL: What? Now? I thought she lived in Winnipeg.

CYRIL: Well, not entirely. Better get dressed. She phoned from the corner.

VAL: WHAT!

CYRIL tosses VAL some clothes, a black pullover and black jeans. VAL puts the pullover on and runs around in a panic. She searches for her new glasses. VAL puts on the jeans. They are very tight and she has a hard time getting into them.

CYRIL: There's something I should tell you. During the time our parents returned to us, Sam went to a therapist because she couldn't create, anymore.

VAL: She's an artist?

CYRIL: Sort of. Anyway, the therapist unblocked her and she had a recovered memory.

VAL: Of what?

CYRIL: Well, she's not sure. Someone abused her. She thinks it's a male. Of course, Dad was the most likely suspect.

VAL: That's awful. Was your father cruel to you, as well?

CYRIL: No. Dad's a really sweet guy.

VAL: Why do you think he did it, then?

CYRIL: He fit the Personality Profile. It's always the people you least suspect. Life was pretty tense at our house what with Dad protesting his innocence and Mum warning all the grandchildren to stay away from him.

VAL: Grandchildren?

CYRIL: Andrea's. My other sister.

VAL: *(relieved)* Oh.

CYRIL: But the most incriminating evidence was The Box of Photos. Photos of Sam that Dad kept in a cardboard box under the bed. Of course, there were photos of me and Andrea there too but still....

VAL: Nude photos?

CYRIL: No. Just regular shots. One of Sam on her horse.

VAL: She used to ride?

CYRIL: Yeah.

VAL: Was she one of those girls who loved horses? Horse wallpaper....

CYRIL: *(joining in)* Horse statuettes, horse bedsheets.... *(pause)* Yes, my sister is a tormented woman.

VAL: I'm sorry but I just don't think your father did it. He says he didn't do it. He's got a box of photos of all you kids. They're normal photos.

CYRIL: Well, we thought about that. And it was pretty unpleasant for us all. So we all decided that our horrible lecherous Uncle Calvin did it. To hell with personality profiles, he's the guy.

VAL: It probably was Uncle Calvin.

CYRIL: Probably. He was always feeling us up.

There is a knock at the door.

CYRIL: Oh God, she's here. And I haven't got to the main part—

CYRIL opens the door. "SAM" stands there, surrounded by boxes and suitcases. "SAM" is SONDRA. SONDRA now looks almost identical to VAL. She has short-cropped dyed blonde hair and wears glasses that are the same style as VAL's new ones. She is about the same height as VAL but much thinner. SAM's persona is much gruffer than SONDRA's. She is cold and distant. She acts with absolute authority.

SAM: Baby!

CYRIL: Sammy! Hey!

    They embrace. VAL stares at "SAM."

CYRIL: Sam, this is Val.

VAL: *(to CYRIL)* That's Sondra.

SAM: *(to CYRIL)* Like her glasses.

VAL: Sondra. Your Stalker.

    "SAM" and CYRIL exchange a look and laugh nervously.

CYRIL: This is Sam.

VAL: It's not Sam, goddamnit! It's Sondra!

CYRIL: Multiple personalities. Sexual abuse. Revisitation Disorder.

VAL: What?!

CYRIL: I'll explain later.

VAL: Why am I dressed like her? Why do we have the same awful haircut?

CYRIL: Sam, why don't you and Drew move your stuff in?

VAL: Drew?! There's more of them? They're staying here?!

    A skinny man, ANDREW, with short cropped dyed blonde hair and also wearing black, barges through the front door. He drops two cat carriers at SAM's feet. He looks familiar. He sees VAL and instantly freezes.

VAL: Is this some cult? Have I joined a cult?

SAM: That's Titus. And that's Andronicus.

VAL: Oh, cats! How nice. Two of them.

SAM: And this is Drew.

VAL: *(to ANDREW)* You know, you look very fam—

> *ANDREW does not wait for her to finish. He nods and runs out to get more bags.*

VAL: …miliar.

SAM: *(to CYRIL, ignoring VAL)* Drew's in hiding. Some bad scene. Biker shit, from the sound of it.

VAL: We might have Hell's Angels dropping by, then?

SAM: I don't think they've found him. Yet.

> *SAM leaves to help ANDREW. CYRIL hauls VAL off to one side.*

CYRIL: There's two of them.

VAL: I hate cats.

CYRIL: Not the cats, my sister! She has two personalities. Sam is my sister. Sondra is a personality that Sam created for self-protection.

VAL: Protection from what?

CYRIL: Well, we're not sure. It's complicated.

SAM and ANDREW come in with more stuff. CYRIL motions for VAL to be quiet. ANDREW is hauling a huge ungainly object, very large, covered with knobs and electrically threatening.

VAL: *(backing away)* What's that?

ANDREW: *(huffs something unintelligible)* Hhhhhmphlihigher.

SAM: *(barks out orders)* Over there, Drew. *(points to an area)*

> *ANDREW staggers over to the area and plonks the object down with a heavy thud*

SAM: Drew used to be in a rock band. Drewly and the Halfwits.

VAL: Maybe that's where—

ANDREW: Performance art. Not a band.

SAM: You played music.

ANDREW: *(defensively)* We weren't trying to.

VAL: *(points to object)* What is that?

SAM: Amplifier. It doesn't work. They're much smaller, now.

ANDREW: The new ones are this big. *(makes a 4 inch by 6 inch motion with his hand)*

VAL: If it doesn't work, then why—

SAM: Drew likes to collect stuff.

ANDREW: This knob here. *(points to a small knob)* It works.

ANDREW and SAM leave to get more stuff.

VAL: How long are they staying here?

CYRIL: Hard to say. But please, be nice to her. If Sam feels threatened, Sondra appears. Sondra turned up last time because I told Sam I was getting married to you.

VAL: Is she likely to flip back into Sondra? I didn't like Sondra much.

CYRIL: Sondra liked you.

VAL: Oh. Sorry. *(pause)* What about the travel agency?

CYRIL: What about it?

VAL: How does she work if she's two people?

CYRIL: They know she has two names. Besides, she only works there part-time.

VAL: Oh, well, part-time. Wait a minute, you said Sam lived in Winnipeg.

CYRIL: Sondra probably told you that Sam lived in Winnipeg.

VAL: Why did you try and get me to look like her?

CYRIL: I thought it would help. If you looked like her, she wouldn't feel threatened.

VAL: I thought it was some sort of sexual turn-on for you.

CYRIL: *(laughs nervously)* Really?

> *SAM and ANDREW come in with more furniture.*

VAL: Wouldn't it be simpler to leave all this stuff in the van? You might find a house right away.

SAM: Cyril's found us a place.

VAL: *(relieved)* Oh! That's great.

SAM: Yeah. *(smiles and grabs CYRIL around the waist)* We'll be moving in a few months.

VAL: What!

CYRIL: I'll go help Drew. *(starts to leave)*

> *VAL starts to follow him.*

SAM: Where's the spare bedroom?

VAL: We don't have one.

CYRIL: You'll be using the living room. *(leaves)*

> *VAL tries to follow CYRIL but is blocked by ANDREW who comes in hauling an enormous speaker.*

SAM: You don't have a TV.

VAL: No. I hate television. Aren't speakers supposed to be small, now?

SAM: Drew! We need the TV and the VCR.

ANDREW nods and huffs. SAM and ANDREW leave to bring in more stuff. CYRIL comes in, hauling another enormous speaker.

VAL: *(runs over and hisses at him)* Months?! How many months?! Why didn't you tell me!!

CYRIL: I told her the house wasn't going to be ready for a while. How was I to know she'd leave immediately.

VAL: She got evicted, didn't she.

CYRIL: Well—

VAL: And you said she could stay with us?

CYRIL: Well—yeah for a week or so.

VAL: And the halfwit?

CYRIL: Hey! I didn't know about him. But it'll be all right. We'll have a great time. My sister's a lot of fun.

VAL: Really? She seems sort of remote.

CYRIL: You'll have to be nice to her. We've been very careful with her. She eats comfort food: Kraft Dinner, Cheezies, potato chips, chocolate pudding.

VAL: She's so thin.

CYRIL: She throws it all up behind the couch. Oh yeah. *(picks up pen and paper to write something down)* Kitty litter box and barf bucket.

VAL: Jesus.

CYRIL: TV's a comfort to her. Only happy family sitcoms. Of course, she has no idea she's sick.

VAL: No?

CYRIL: She thinks she's a brilliant conceptual artist setting some sort of retro-trend. Part of her art.

VAL: Is she going to watch TV every night?

CYRIL: She likes TV.

VAL: But not too late. I have to get up early—

> *SAM comes in. She clutches the television to her as if it were a holy relic. The living room should now be filled with electronic equipment, suitcases, boxes etc. SAM caresses the television.*

CYRIL: Val, why don't you offer Sam something?

VAL: Sorry. Sam, you must be really tired after all that driving. Can I get you something? A cup of coffee? Tea?

SAM: No. Are you an air hostess?

VAL: No.

SAM: You look like an air hostess. That stupid paste-on smile they have.

VAL: Stewardesses don't smile, anymore. Haven't you noticed?

SAM: It's the concept, not the reality, that's important. The concept. *(sings)* Fly, the friendly skies....

CYRIL: *(whispers)* My sister's in trauma.

VAL: Again? Didn't she just come out of trauma?

SAM: *(shrieks)* Winnipeg! I came out of Winnipeg!

VAL: *(dumbfounded)* Well, I guess I'll make some tea. Cyril, you'd like tea?

CYRIL: *(flashes her a winning smile)* Please, darling.

SAM: Yeah. Ship your stupid bourgeois pig face oudda here!

VAL: What!

CYRIL: *(tries to usher VAL quickly out the door)* Sam's just disappointed that you're leaving. She connected with you.

SAM: OINK! OINK! Oink Oink!

> *VAL reappears from the kitchen. She looks very annoyed. Her attention is suddenly drawn to ANDREW who comes in, carrying a very heavy box. It lands with a thud.*

VAL: Oh, books.

ANDREW: No—not books—definitely not books. *(guards box from VAL)*

VAL: So, how long have you known Sam?

ANDREW: Ooh—it's—ah—been two days now.

VAL: Oh. Long time.

SAM: Drew! Help Cyril!

SAM, ANDREW and CYRIL leave to bring in the rest of the stuff. VAL examines the box.

VAL: *(pulling out books) How to Fill the Empty Space* by Vladimir Bolunk. *Crime and Punishment (muses) Crime and Punishment (opens inside of book and reads)* Metro Civic Library—Rosehill Branch. Drew, Drew....

ANDREW, CYRIL and SAM come in with more boxes.

SAM: Well, that about covers it. We'll leave the rest of the stuff in the van.

VAL stares at ANDREW. She suddenly recognizes him.

VAL: ANDREW BLETT! YOU'RE ANDREW BLETT, AREN'T YOU!

ANDREW: Oh God. Bad Karma or what.

VAL: THIS MAN IS A D.B.!

ANDREW: Try and make a clean break and the past comes back to haunt you.

CYRIL: A D. what?

ANDREW: Delinquent Borrower. *(to VAL)* I'm returning them. HONEST! They're in the box, all packed up and ready to go.

VAL: Chatting me up in the library, flirting with me....

CYRIL: Chatting you up?

VAL: Just to get the books!

CYRIL: Flirting with you?

VAL: *(imitates ANDREW)* "What sort of fiend would do that." You're the fiend!

ANDREW: Honest! It wasn't me. Some other fiend stole those books. I stole these books.

VAL: I will not have this D.B. in my house!

CYRIL: *(to ANDREW)* What were you doing with Val?

ANDREW: Nothing! I don't mean to steal books. I can't help it. I'm a kleptomaniac.

VAL: No, you're not. You're a thief!

ANDREW: No really, I'm a kleptomaniac. It's an illness.

VAL: Don't give me that bullshit about illness. THIEF! THIEF!

ANDREW: I have this fixation. A fetish, I guess. It's not really books but books are a symptom. It's actually anything to do with libraries. *(embarrassed)* I have a fetish for librarians.

SAM: You have got to be joking.

ANDREW: I wish I were. It's a very embarrassing fetish. People can relate to foot fetishes. Shoe fetishes, hats, gloves but librarians! It's humiliating.

VAL: I like to think a librarian is slightly more active than a hat or a glove.

ANDREW: To a fetishist, it's all the same.

VAL: Thanks. Now I feel really attractive.

CYRIL: This is fascinating. How do you get a fetish?

ANDREW: It just happens. I was little. I was in the library. Didn't feel anything odd. But I was in between two stacks of books and suddenly I saw this tweed skirt—

VAL: Oh pullease!

ANDREW: Right in front of me, sort of hidden behind the books. It was Miss Grimshaw. She didn't know I was there. She was adjusting her stockings and she lifted up her skirt. She was wearing a garter belt! And I just lost it. I sort of fainted in a rapture and I've been hooked ever since. But you know, it's good to have a fetish. We are the lucky ones.

SAM: This calls for a celebration!

> *SAM brandishes an electric hair clipper. A buzzing sound is heard, similar to the buzzing sound of the first scene.*

SAM: A new start! *(proceeds to shave her head)*

VAL: God.

ACT TWO

Scene 1

> *A week later. SAM, ANDREW and CYRIL are on rollerblades. SAM is holding a buzzing razor and ordering ANDREW and CYRIL about. VAL walks in. She is wearing her brown Fortrel uniform. She is ignored by the others.*

SAM: *(to ANDREW)* I need some rope. *(rolls offstage)*

ANDREW: I could hold him down.

SAM: *(off)* Hurry! Do we have a muzzle?

CYRIL: I could use one of Val's scarves. *(starts to roll off to get it)*

> *Buzzing sounds offstage. VAL grabs CYRIL as he rolls by.*

VAL: We hardly see each other these days.

CYRIL: Back in a sec. *(skates off)*

ANDREW: *(suddenly notices what VAL is wearing)* What is that?

VAL: My uniform.

ANDREW: God! They are systematically destroying everything I hold sacred. I can't even get remotely aroused looking at that.

VAL: I don't WANT you to get aroused.

CYRIL skates by, holding one of VAL's scarves.

ANDREW: Why do they do that? They keep changing all the uniforms. Why can't everyone keep the same uniform? There's probably a gas station attendant wearing tweed skirt and brogues. *(looks at her closely)* What made you decide to become a librarian?

VAL: Are we going to continue like this indefinitely?

ANDREW: What?

VAL: Every time you see me, you ask me some dumb library question. Let's get it over with, okay?

ANDREW: Okay. What's it like being a librarian?

VAL: I don't know. It's a job.

ANDREW: Does the fact that you'll never get married bother you?

VAL: I am married.

ANDREW: Really. Who to?

VAL: Cyril! The man whose apartment you've laid siege to. The man whose sister you're banging.

ANDREW: We're not banging.

VAL: No?

ANDREW: No. She's not into it.

VAL: Do you think it's genetic?

ANDREW: What?

VAL: Nothing.

ANDREW: I thought you were his other sister.

VAL: You thought I was his sister?!

ANDREW: How do you feel about the Dewey Decimal System?

VAL: I don't have any feelings about it.

ANDREW: Don't you guys sit around and make Dewey Decimal jokes.

VAL: WHAT IS THE MATTER WITH YOU!

ANDREW: Geez, cranky. It's a simple question.

VAL: It's a stupid question. What sort of jokes could you make about a bunch of numbers. 158 point 6. HA! HA! HA! 392 point 549. HO! HO! HO!

ANDREW: Okay Okay.

VAL: Do you have any more stupid clichéd questions to ask!

ANDREW: Do you see yourself as an Authority Figure?

VAL: No.

ANDREW tries to look at VAL's back

VAL: *(glances behind her)* Is there something on my back?

ANDREW: So, you're not the Head Librarian.

VAL: No.

ANDREW: *(smiles knowingly)* Ah yes.

VAL: What?

ANDREW: It's just a little something I've noticed. I've been at the larger branches. City Hall, Yorkville, Forest Hill and it's an odd thing. Nothing really. The Head Librarians have very straight backs.

VAL: Yeah?

ANDREW: But the second-in-command has a slight hump. And as you go down the line of authority, they get more and more bent over.

SAM: *(off)* DREW!!

VAL: Are you saying I've got a HUMPBACK!! *(lunges at him)*

ANDREW: *(dodges her and skates out of the room)* Sorry.

> CYRIL *tries to skate past VAL. VAL grabs him as he goes by.*

VAL: I can't take much more of this.

CYRIL: What?

VAL: The noise, the chaos, the confusion. The constant buzzing. What the hell is she shaving now!

CYRIL: The neighbour's collie.

VAL: The neighbour's collie?!

CYRIL: He came into our yard.

VAL: Oh God! Do they know? Are we all going to be arrested?

CYRIL: Sam's exploring purity of line.

VAL: That's going to be our defense? Uh, sorry your honour, we were exploring purity of line.

CYRIL: It's no big deal.

VAL: No big deal! She did the neighbourhood cats last week. People are going to start to get mad.

CYRIL: They're already mad. They just don't know who's doing it.

VAL: Great! And does she have to have the TV on all day and all night?

CYRIL: You don't like her.

VAL: She hasn't spoken to me since she's invaded. We're never alone. I used to complain about sex. I don't even sleep with you, now. You're in the living room, packed up like sardines watching reruns of *Leave it to Beaver*. Is your sister a coke addict?

CYRIL: Of course not.

VAL: It's so weird. Drug culture without the drugs.

CYRIL: Sam can't relate to straights.

VAL: Straights.

CYRIL: People with regular jobs.

VAL: You have a regular job. She relates to you.

CYRIL: I'm a professor. It doesn't count. Now that I have tenure, I can be as demented as I like.

VAL: You've been restraining yourself?!

CYRIL: I'm sorry you don't like my sister.

VAL: Honey, I'm trying to like her but she acts as if I weren't here.

SAM: *(off)* CYRIL!

> *CYRIL skates off. VAL is so involved in her explanation that she doesn't notice.*

VAL: As if I were a slightly animate object. Say, a fish. Not half as interesting as a cat, but alive. Yes. A fish. *(looks up)* Cyril? *(sees that she is alone)*

> *Sounds of CYRIL and SAM laughing together offstage.*

Scene 2

VAL and MARGE in the van.

VAL: It's all so weird. I don't even get to talk to him,
anymore. And the TV. It's on all day and all night. ALL
NIGHT. And it's not just regular TV. It's the
SHOPPING CHANNEL! It doesn't matter how low they
turn it down. In fact, I think it's worse 'cause I can't
quite make out what's being said. *(does an imitation of the
Shopping Channel turned down low)* And that drives me
crazy. I hear bits and pieces and I stay up trying to
figure out what I'm supposed to buy. A month of sleep
deprivation. I'm starting to crack up, Marge. I'm
starting to lose it. I think he might be in love with his
sister. Isn't that nuts?! *(laughs too hysterically)* Of course,
I'm sure nothing bad is going on. They're just close. It's
an English thing to do. Fall in love with your sister.
Wordsworth and his sister. Charles and Mary Lamb.
Bramwell Bronte...and all his sisters. Must have been
that English boarding school he went to. I'm sure he
doesn't mean it? Do you think he means it? What
should I do if he means it?

MARGE: You know, just because my name's Marge doesn't
mean you can come to me with all your personal
problems.

VAL: What?

MARGE: People are always telling me their personal shit. It
bores the hell out of me.

VAL: Sorry. I just wanted to know what you'd do.

MARGE: Virginia Woolf!

VAL: What?

MARGE: Get it on with the sister.

VAL: Thanks. You're a lot of help.

MARGE: Well, you're not getting any action out of your husband. That's so sad.

VAL: It's all right, Marge. You don't need to pretend to be sympathetic.

MARGE: I mean, doesn't it make you wonder if there's some pheromone you're giving off.

VAL: This isn't helping me, Marge.

MARGE: Some people just kill sexual desire, you know. You think they're sexy when you meet them. You get to know them and it just ends. Maybe you're one of those.

VAL: You know those movies and plays where there's the really nice lesbian?

MARGE: The what?

VAL: The really nice lesbian who's a complete saint. She's infatuated with the hetero woman who's had a bad time with men. This lesbian is always understanding. Always there to lend moral support. Everything the hetero woman does is sublime truth. You know that lesbian?

MARGE: No. She sounds like an asshole.

VAL: Lesbians are supposed to be understanding.

MARGE: I don't know what book you read but it's not my
  genre. What happens in the end of those plays?

VAL: Oh. Well, you know. *(uncomfortable pause)* You are not
  a saint, Marge. I may be a screwed-up hetero woman
  but you are a long way from being a saint. And it only
  works if the lesbian is a saint.

MARGE: You don't say? I wasn't thinking of me. Were you
  thinking of me that way for a while now?

VAL: No!

MARGE: You're sure about that.

VAL: Yes!

MARGE: Look, I'm just trying to figure out what's wrong
  with you.

VAL: There's nothing wrong with me!

MARGE: There might be. Your husband doesn't want to
  sleep with you.

VAL: THAT'S IT! LET'S GET THIS PRICKHEAD!

MARGE: Who?

VAL: WHOEVER'S ON YOUR LIST! Let's get him. I'm in
  the mood now.

MARGE: *(jabs at a name in her folder)* Andrew Blett!

VAL: What!

MARGE: He's been sighted. In your area. I have an address— *(starts to flip through file)*

VAL: Really? Hasn't he returned the books? I thought he returned them.

MARGE: Do you know something about this guy?

VAL: *(hastily)* Oh no. No.

MARGE: He was lurking around Spadina Branch this morning. 'Course they couldn't do anything about it. We're the only people authorized to take out D.B.s.

VAL: "Take out?"

MARGE: I haven't shown you that procedure, yet.

VAL: Let's not do him. Not today.

MARGE: *(flips a page)* Well, we could go for the U. of T. professor. He's cleaned out our entire collection of deconstructivist literature. Not that that's a great loss.

VAL: Perfect. Let's get him. What's his name?

MARGE: Cyril something. *(flips through file)*

VAL: Cyril?

MARGE: Cyril Wynton-Smith.

VAL: AAAAGH!

MARGE: What.

VAL: That's my husband. Except it's Smythe, not Smith.

MARGE: You sure?

VAL: How many Cyril Winton-Smythes can there be?

MARGE: I was sure it was Wynton-Smith. 561 Palmerston Avenue?

VAL: Doesn't ring a bell. We've not exactly been close lately. Maybe he's moved out and I haven't noticed.

MARGE: Well, let's get him. Maybe this one likes sex. Sorry.

Scene 3

MARGE and VAL in front of a house.

MARGE: *(banging on door)* OPEN UP IN THERE!!

VAL: You know, Marge. Have you ever thought of just knocking sometime.

MARGE: Knocking?

VAL: Yeah, nicely—like a salesperson. Knock in such a way that they'll open the door. Freely. Innocently.

MARGE: *(pauses, considers it)* Wouldn't work. *(bangs on door)* MR. CYRIL WINTON-SMYTHE. WE HAVE A WARRANT FOR YOUR ARREST.

> *A man pokes his head out of an upstairs window. He looks exactly like CYRIL but he is dressed in a smoking jacket and a cravat. He has a pronounced English accent.*

VAL: *(gasps)* Cyril!

CYRIL X: Smith. Not Smythe. Wynton. Not Winton. *(pokes head back in)*

MARGE: OPEN UP!! OR WE'LL BUST THE DOOR DOWN.

VAL: This is really humiliating.

CYRIL X: *(steps out, closes door behind him quickly)* Where's your warrant?

MARGE: Ah—

VAL: Cyril!

CYRIL X: Yes.

VAL: It's me.

> *CYRIL X looks blank.*

VAL: Val. *(pause)* Your wife.

CYRIL X: Oh Christ! *(goes back in and slams the door, bolts it)*

MARGE: And you say he doesn't want to have sex with you.

VAL: CYRRRRRIIIILL!!!!! *(bangs on door)*

MARGE: I want those books, Buster!

CYRIL X: *(pokes head out window)* You don't have a warrant. Go away or I'll call the police.

VAL: Cyril, if you have any respect for our marriage, you'll talk to—

CYRIL X: I have no idea who you are, madam, but I swear I did not marry you. Not in a blue moon. Not in a drunken stupor. Not in a fit of delirium. Not at any time! You are not my wife. GO AWAY! *(slams window)*

MARGE: He seems pretty firm on that point. *(starts to walk around the side of the house)* Well, we'll have to use the alternative approach. B. & E.

VAL: Break and Enter?! Now?!

MARGE: You're right. Now's a bad time. He'll be expecting us. Later.

They walk away.

VAL: He's the spitting image. Same name even. Cyril never mentioned that he had a twin. Why would they have the same name?

MARGE: Unimaginative parents?

VAL: They must be twins.

MARGE: It seems harsh to name someone Cyril twice.

Scene 4

> *VAL's apartment. VAL enters. ANDREW is sitting on the couch. He is reading a book.*

VAL: *(calls)* C-Y-R-I-L! C-Y-R-I-L!

ANDREW: He and Sam are outside in the back.

VAL: Another dog?

> *ANDREW is about to answer.*

VAL: No. Don't tell me. I don't want to know. *(looks around)* My God, it's actually quiet in here. The TV's not on. *(looks at ANDREW)* You're reading a book.

ANDREW: Yes.

VAL: I didn't know you read books. I thought you just stole them.

ANDREW: No. It's a process. I steal them and then I read them.

VAL: I know this will complicate your process but why don't you sign them out on your library card, read them and then return them to the library where you got them?

> *ANDREW looks blankly at her. SAM enters. with CYRIL slightly behind. They are wearing rollerblades. SAM does not acknowledge VAL.*

VAL: Hi, Sam. Nice to see you. How have you been? Fine? Well, that's nice.

SAM: Oink! Oink! OINK! OINK! *(turns around and rolls back into the kitchen)*

VAL: Does she have to do that?

CYRIL: It's how she—

VAL: I know, I know. Cyril, the most bizarre thing happened. I met a man who looks just like you.

CYRIL: We're out of Kraft Dinner.

VAL: He could be your twin. Same name and everything. Well, not quite the same name. Wynton-Smith. He's a professor at U. of T. as well.

CYRIL: If Sam doesn't get Kraft Dinner, she'll go berserk.

VAL: Honey, she's already there. Have you heard a word I said? I met your twin!

CYRIL: Yes. I know. A real English twit.

VAL: You've met him?!

CYRIL: I grew up with him. Stupid little Anglophile.

VAL: You never told me you had a twin brother.

CYRIL: That's because I hate his guts.

VAL: Your parents named you both Cyril?!

CYRIL: No. His name is Lyle. He didn't like his name. He thought I had a better name. Everything I had, he wanted, so he took my name, too.

ANDREW: I'm a little confused. You have a twin brother. You teach at the same university and you don't talk to each other?!

CYRIL: I'm in the Mathematics Department. He's in Psychology.

ANDREW: Oh. Well, that explains it.

VAL: Is he a genius as well?

CYRIL: No. He's dumb as a post.

VAL: He's a Psychology professor.

CYRIL: I rest my case.

VAL: There are all these things you're not telling me. Do you have any other brothers and sisters that I should know about? Any other family members?

CYRIL: Really darling, it's not important.

VAL: I'd like to meet your brother.

CYRIL: You have met him.

VAL: Have him for dinner. Something like that.

> *SAM comes in. She is now dressed in sexually provocative, if somewhat bizarre, clothes. She is no longer wearing her rollerblades. She pushes CYRIL onto the couch and starts removing his rollerblades in a very seductive manner.*

VAL: *(feebly, pretending not to notice)* What about your other sister? The nice one? When am I going to meet her?

SAM: Let's dance!

CYRIL: Now?

SAM: Yeah! Or have you forgotten?

SAM gets up and puts some music on.

SAM: *(starts dancing)* Come on, baby. Let's dance!

CYRIL starts dancing with SAM. ANDREW and VAL look puzzled. They sit off to one side and watch CYRIL and SAM dance. They dance in an overtly sexual manner. They do not take their eyes off each other the entire time they dance. They counter each other's moves in an uncanny way.

VAL: They—ah—dance very well together.

ANDREW: Uh—yeah.

VAL: I'd never dance that way with my brother. Would you?

ANDREW: I don't know your brother. Oh. Sorry. No. No, I wouldn't. Dance that way.

VAL: I don't have a brother.

ANDREW: I don't have a sister. *(pause)* I don't want a sister.

VAL: Me, neither.

ANDREW: Do you really want to meet the rest of his family?

They look at each other.

ANDREW: Do you want to dance?

VAL: Oh—well—not really.

ANDREW: Would you rather sit and watch them?

VAL: You have a point.

They get up to dance. The music changes to a slow dance. SAM puts out her hand seductively and draws CYRIL close to her. They dance as two people in love. ANDREW and VAL dance awkwardly together. They watch SAM and CYRIL.

Scene 5

SAM is stuffing Cheezies into her mouth and shaving the legs of an assortment of Barbie dolls. VAL walks in.

VAL: *(shouts to be heard above the razor)* You know, you've been here for over a month now and we've never really had a conversation.

SAM: *(can't hear)* A WHAT?

VAL: A CONVERSATION.

VAL motions for SAM to turn the razor off. SAM does so reluctantly. During VAL's "conversation," SAM tortures the Barbie dolls.

VAL: I thought maybe we might have hurt your feelings. I always felt Cyril and I should have told your family but Cyril said he didn't have a family so that made it difficult—

SAM: Told my family what?

VAL: About the marriage.

SAM: What marriage?

VAL: Our marriage. Cyril and I.

SAM: Cyril would never marry someone like you. He loves me.

VAL: He what?

SAM: I'm sure he's fond of you.

VAL: He married me!

SAM: These days, that's no proof of anything.

VAL: How long do you plan to be staying with us?

SAM: We're splitting the rent. It's a shared home, now.

VAL: I wasn't aware your staying here was a permanent condition.

SAM: I wasn't aware your marriage was a permanent condition.

VAL: You are living in my home. I feel you should make some effort to get along.

SAM: Why? You are insignificant to me. Cyril loves me. He always has and he always will. Girlfriends, wives....

VAL: Wives?

SAM: ...Are simply meaningless interludes in his process of self-denial. Shouldn't you be at work? All you bourgeoisie work, don't you?

VAL: Yeah. Do you work? Do you do anything? Have a job? Something that might actually take you out of my home for eight hours at a time. Anything like that?

SAM: I'm a conceptual artist. I work in my head.

VAL: That pays the rent?

SAM: It's a cheap head. *(slight pause)* Oh, money. You meant money. I teach at universities.

VAL: You teach.

SAM: Yes.

VAL: You teach innocent young people how to be like you.

SAM: They're not so innocent.

VAL: This is the most depressing conversation I've ever had in my life.

SAM: You've led a sheltered life. I suppose you plan to move into our new home with us, then? Keep up appearances.

VAL: Pardon?

SAM: To be with your "husband."

VAL: Cyril's moving in with you?!

SAM: Yes. Didn't he tell you? He's bad that way. Probably didn't think it was important.

VAL: *(calls out)* C-Y-R-R-I-L!

SAM: He's gone to Winnipeg. Conference.

VAL: Winnipeg? How long's he going to be away for?

SAM: As long as he likes. You know professors.

VAL: No. I don't, apparently. I don't know anyone. *(heads out the door in a bewildered and defeated manner)*

Just as VAL is about to go out the door, she walks headlong into a woman.

SNARPLES: Hello. My name is Evelyn Snarples. I'm your next door neighbour.

VAL: Oh—hello.

SNARPLES: I'm glad you answered the door. I've come by several times and no one answers the door.

VAL: It's true. People don't answer doors, anymore.

SNARPLES: Then I slipped a note under your door for someone to call me. But no one called.

VAL: I know. People don't read notes, anymore, either.

SNARPLES: Well, at least you answered the door.

VAL: Actually, I didn't. I was just on my way out and you happened to be here. *(tries to get by)*

SNARPLES: *(pins VAL to the door)* It's about McTavish.

VAL: McWho?

SNARPLES: My collie. McTavish.

SAM walks by. She turns on the razor and smiles menacingly.

SNARPLES: You see, he was shaved. Shaved to his skin.

VAL: Really?

SNARPLES: *(trying to push past VAL)* We didn't even know it was our dog. He looked like a big rat. He was very upset. And now he won't leave the house.

VAL: Oh.

SNARPLES: Yes. Collies are very sensitive dogs. He's been publicly humiliated and I want to find the perpetrator! *(pushes past)* You! You there!

SAM: *(stops)* Yeah.

SNARPLES: Did you shave my dog?

SAM: Who wants to know?

SNARPLES: Who do you think wants to know! I do! I just asked you! *(to VAL)* She shaved my dog, didn't she.

VAL: Yes. She did.

SAM: Your dog was trespassing.

SNARPLES: Well, McTavish might have wandered but he would never trespass.

SAM: He disobeyed the leash law.

SNARPLES: I'll take you to court.

SAM: You don't have a case.

SNARPLES: Abduction! Abduction and Defilement! Mrs. Van Roggen is very upset about her cat.

SAM: I admit nothing. *(pushes MRS. SNARPLES out the door)*

SNARPLES: *(protesting)* We'll call the police!

SAM: *(slams door, bolts it, turns on VAL)* YOU! You set her after me! *(turns on shaver, raises it)*

VAL: Oh God— *(turns to run)*

>   *SAM grabs VAL and tries to pin her down so she can shave her head. They struggle. Just as SAM is about to shave VAL's hair, VAL is able to shut the razor off. SAM suddenly stops and looks at VAL.*

SAM: Hi.

VAL: Hi?

SAM: *(looks at herself, feels her head)* Oh God! It happened again. I'm so embarrassed. *(gets off VAL, heads toward couch, fumbles around behind one of the seats)* I guess Cyril called them to say I wouldn't be in to work for a while. They're very understanding.

VAL: They?

SAM: Aunt Betty and Uncle Calvin. They run it.

VAL: It?

SAM: The travel agency. How long was I gone this time?

VAL: Sondra?

SONDRA: *(pulls out a black wig from the couch, plonks it on her head)* Hiya, kiddo.

VAL: I'm a little confused.

SONDRA: You're confused. Try living with it.

VAL: I have. Believe me, I have.

SONDRA: Sam's a real bitch I've been told. Course I'm never around to see her. She's my alternate.

VAL: No—no—you are Sam's alternate personality.

SONDRA: Did Cyril tell you that? Oh God, he's awful. He's such a liar.

VAL: Don't start with me.

SONDRA: When I was married to Cyril, he was in love with his sister, Andrea.

VAL: When you were what?!

SONDRA: He kept trying to get me to look like Andrea— of course—then she had jet black hair like Cleopatra. So I had to have jet black hair like Cleopatra. And blue kohl eyeshadow. Andrea had god-awful taste. The tension kept building and building till finally I just snapped. I became his sister. His perfect sister, Sam.

VAL: You weren't perfect. You were really far from perfect.

SONDRA: Anyway, it's nice to be back. Did you miss me?

VAL: Compared to what.

SONDRA: Aw come on, you missed me.

VAL: I'm delighted that you're back. Because now I can throw you out! *(starts to push SONDRA out the door)* I'll arrange to have your things dropped off. *(almost has SONDRA out the door)*

SONDRA: There's just one thing. The divorce.

VAL: Look, what goes on between Cyril and me is our business. First, I have to find him. Then we'll have a talk. Then I'll enroll him in a Liar's therapy workshop—

SONDRA: There was no divorce.

VAL: And there will be no divorce. Not until I've heard his side.

SONDRA: Between us. Cyril and me. No divorce. Get it? I'm still married to him. He's a bigamist.

VAL: A what?

SONDRA: *(looks around)* Nice place you have here. I might be back late. Double shift. *(leaves)*

> VAL collapses in a chair. She accidentally sits on the remote switch which turns on the TV. VAL sits up with a start as the TV show goes on. She wanders out of the room, muttering to herself. Focus on the TV.

TV JEAN: Well, Oprah, I'm basically a nice person. And very patient. Patient and understanding. But Ron had been abusing me for a long time.

TV OPRAH: Did he beat you?

TV JEAN: No—no—worse than that. Mental abuse. Everything I did was wrong. Little things. That's how it started. I didn't dress right. I was too fat. My hair was wrong. Even my glasses. I changed my prescription but it turned out he meant the frames. He tried to murder me. Mentally. He kept turning the gas further and further down but my little personal pilot light wouldn't go out.

TV OPRAH: Jean, level with me. What made you do it?

TV JEAN: I don't know. I'd always kept my temper in check. Never got mad. But somehow when I saw the two of them in bed together, I guess I just lost it.

> VAL *wanders back in. She can either be changed or in the process of putting on her library clothes—skirt, blouse, flat shoes. She carries her cardigan, holding it close to her, like a security blanket.*

TV OPRAH: Jean, you shot their heads off.

> VAL *looks up.*

TV JEAN: What can I say? I had no idea I was going to do that.

OPRAH: Jean.

JEAN: It was a misfire. I meant to shoot myself.

TV OPRAH: Jean, you went to their home.

TV JEAN: My home! It used to be my home! He was my husband and she took him!!

TV OPRAH: Sorry—your old home. You go there at five in the morning with a sawed-off shotgun.

TV JEAN: I wanted to talk to them.

TV OPRAH: With a gun?!

TV JEAN: The gun was so they'd listen.

TV OPRAH: But you killed them.

TV JEAN: Yes and I feel badly about that but I guess we have to admit our mistakes and move on in this life.

TV OPRAH: Must be a different life here in the Women's Correctional Facility.

TV JEAN: Actually, it's a lot like home. Once a housewife, always a housewife. I like to tidy the cell and straighten out the lockers....

> *VAL snaps off the television and sits alone, brooding in the dark. ANDREW comes in. He turns on the light and is very surprised to see VAL.*

ANDREW: Oh! Ah—hi—

VAL: She's not here.

ANDREW: I wasn't looking for her.

VAL: No. I mean she's really NOT HERE. She's out. Worse than out, in fact. She's Sondra.

ANDREW: *(not understanding)* Sondra.

VAL: Sondra! Her other personality.

ANDREW: She has two?

VAL: Yes. Of course!

ANDREW: I hadn't noticed. *(looks at VAL)* You're—ah—in your library clothes.

VAL: It's what I wear when I'm depressed.

ANDREW: It's—ah—the entire ensemble.

VAL: It's what I am. A spinster librarian. From my head to my toes.

ANDREW: You're married.

VAL: I might not be. Sondra has just informed me that Cyril is her husband. Her current husband. In honour of the occasion, I'm all decked out in my spinster finery. Like the oxfords? *(flashes her foot at ANDREW)*

ANDREW: Ah—yeah.

VAL: You're just being kind.

ANDREW: No—no. I'm not. *(takes her foot and caresses it)* *(smiles)* Lisle stockings.

VAL: Remember lisle stockings?

ANDREW: Vividly.

VAL: You can still buy them. When I'm feeling really perverse, such as today, I wear them. *(snaps a garter under her skirt)*

> *ANDREW swoons quietly.*

VAL: *(unaware of the effect she is having)* And the tweed skirt? Like the tweed skirt?

ANDREW: *(puts his hand on VAL's skirt)* Oh yes. *(starts running his hands up and down her skirt)*

> *VAL leaps up to get something. ANDREW lurches off the couch. VAL turns around and stands over him. ANDREW is desperately trying to control himself.*

VAL: What's the matter?

ANDREW: *(staring up at her)(grabs VAL's calf and caresses it)* Oh God. Oh God.

VAL: Is something wrong?

ANDREW: Do you have any idea of the effect you're having on me.

VAL: What?

ANDREW: My—ah—disability.

VAL: *(puzzled, goes over to the couch and sits down)* Disability. *(starts to clean her cat's eye glasses which are on a string)* Disability.

ANDREW: *(moans and pounds the floor with his foot)* Self-control. You can conquer this. Self-control. It's all it takes. A little self-control.

> *ANDREW gets up and walks over to the couch. He sits down beside VAL and tries to act nonchalant.*

VAL: Oh yeah, that's what I got up for. To complete the outfit. *(gets up and puts on her cardigan)* La pièce de résistance. The baggy cardigan. This sweater has sat on the back of a chair in an airless library stack for five years. Isn't that exciting?

ANDREW: *(muttering)* Self-control, self-control....

VAL: *(puts out her arm for him to smell)* Book smell.

ANDREW: *(takes VAL's arm and buries his face in it)* Mmmhmm—ahhuh—ahhuh—yeah—right—okay. *(lunges at VAL)*

VAL: *(falling back on the couch)* Oh! That's what you meant. I thought you were missing a limb or something. Your fetish!

ANDREW: *(climbing over VAL's body, caressing her clothes)* Well, fetish is sort of an impersonal term for—um—something which is actually very personal—so—I—ah—prefer to think of my disorder as—ah—an extreme interest. I—ah—am extremely interested in you. *(starts kissing VAL)*

   VAL responds.

ANDREW: *(suddenly stops kissing VAL, sits up)* Oh God! I'm sorry. I shouldn't have done that. That was very male of me. It's been a long time since I've done something male, so you'll have to forgive me. I mean, you could press charges. Women do that now, don't they?

VAL: Yes. They do. *(kisses him)*

ANDREW: *(pulls away)* Enticement! If you press charges, I could say you enticed me.

VAL: Sweet talker.

ANDREW: I mean it.

VAL: I won't press charges, if you won't press charges.

ANDREW: Promise?

>   *ANDREW starts kissing VAL.*

VAL: There's just one thing.

ANDREW: *(in between kisses)* What?

VAL: Are you extremely interested in me or just in my
clothes?

ANDREW: Both!

VAL: Because I want to be desired for myself.

ANDREW: You are! You are!

VAL: *(pushes ANDREW off her)* A test.

>   *VAL takes her sweater off and throws it in a pile on the
>   other side of ANDREW. ANDREW looks at the sweater, looks
>   at VAL, looks at the sweater, looks at VAL. VAL removes her
>   oxfords and puts them on the pile with the sweater. VAL
>   removes her blouse and puts it on the pile. ANDREW gets
>   frantic. He stares at the pile of clothes as they mount up.
>   He stares at VAL as she undresses.*

ANDREW: *(increasingly desperate, finally lunges at VAL)* My
God! I'm cured!

>   *He flings VAL behind the couch. Lights down.*

Scene 6

A few hours later. Lights up. Loud banging on the door.

MARGE'S VOICE: ANDREW BLETT! WE KNOW YOU'RE IN THERE, ANDREW BLETT!!

ANDREW and VAL poke their heads up from behind the couch. They rush to put clothes on.

ANDREW: Oh Christ! It's Sam. It's her other personality.

VAL: Actually, I think I know—

MARGE'S VOICE: COME OUT WITH YOUR HANDS UP!

ANDREW: Before I go out and get crucified, that was magnificent!

VAL: Thanks.

ANDREW: No. Really Magnificent. *(kisses VAL passionately, they tumble back behind the couch)*

MARGE'S VOICE: WE'VE GOT THE HOUSE SURROUNDED!

VAL: I guess I better let her in. She'll just keep yelling until I do.

ANDREW: No, no. I'll face her. Better get it over with. *(gets up, walks over to the door)*

MARGE'S VOICE: I'M GONNA COUNT TO THREE. ONE! TWO!

ANDREW opens the door.

MARGE: THREEEEEEE! *(charges in and grabs ANDREW)*

ANDREW: My God! She's had a makeover.

VAL: This is Marge. The Book Collector.

MARGE: I am the Metropolitan Public Library—Val, what are you doing here? Oh—undercover work, a little Mata Hari, are we. I don't know that I approve of your methods, Val, but it worked. Nice job, Pardner. *(shouts)* UP AGAINST THE WALL, BLETT! SPREAD YOUR LEGS!

ANDREW: What?!

VAL: Marge, calm down. Andrew turned himself in.

ANDREW: I did?

MARGE: What were you doing—going Blett hunting without me!

ANDREW: Blett hunting?

VAL: *(sheepishly)* We live here.

MARGE: What?!

SONDRA walks in.

SONDRA: People are so stupid. *(laughs to herself)* I love my job. I'm one of the few people on this planet who loves her job.

MARGE: I love my job.

SONDRA: You do? Who are you? Another one of Cyril's wives?

MARGE: No. I'm gay.

SONDRA: Well, nice to meet you, Gaye. Make yourself at home.

MARGE: No. I'm a lesbian.

SONDRA: And an unusual one at that, to let Cyril get his hands on you.

MARGE: I've never met Cyril.

SONDRA: Long distance relations. That's the key to a successful marriage. Hey Val! Gaye here is married to Cyril as well. Are you moving in too, Gaye?

MARGE: I'm not GAYE!

SONDRA: You're not happy, Gaye?

MARGE: I'm Lesbian Gay!

SONDRA: Lesbian Gay...Spalding Gay's sister?

MARGE: Gray! Spalding Gray!

SONDRA: Is that Spalding over there? *(starts to walk over to ANDREW)*

VAL: Sondra?

SONDRA: *(looks at VAL)* Yes?

VAL: What do you know about Lyle?

SONDRA: *(frightened)* Lyle?

VAL: Cyril's twin brother. Do you know him?

SONDRA: He's not here, is he? *(starts to get hysterical)* Oh God, is he here!? Is he here??!!!!! No! No! He can't be here!!! Ah—ah—ah! *(faints, falls in a heap)*

MARGE: Well, that shut her up. Nice work, Val.

VAL: How odd.

MARGE: Living with a D.B. and you never told me! You've been harbouring a fugitive.

> *While MARGE, VAL and ANDREW talk, SONDRA regains consciousness. SONDRA feels her head, feels the black wig and throws it away with disdain. She puts her rollerblades on.*

VAL: He promised he wouldn't steal any more books. He's harmless.

ANDREW: I'm an animal. An untamed stallion.

MARGE: *(to BLETT)* Yeah, right. *(to VAL)* Couldn't you have waited for me so we could have both got him.

ANDREW: *(looks at MARGE nervously)* I don't want her.

> *VAL hears the sound of SAM snapping on her rollerblades and looks over at her.*

VAL: Damn! She's come to. *(turns away in disgust)* It's Sam. The other personality.

> *SAM starts skating around the room. MARGE watches her.*

MARGE: *(to VAL)* What's she like?

VAL: Worse. Far worse.

MARGE: *(watching her in fascination)* She seems sort of interesting.

SAM: *(to VAL)* I was going to tell Cyril to start having sex with you. But it's good you've made other arrangements.

ANDREW: I don't think I'm an arrangement, exactly. *(to VAL)* Am I?

VAL: No. Of course not.

SAM: Everyone needs a lover. It reduces tension. *(suddenly skates up to MARGE, stops and stares at her, says dreamily)* Bobby.

MARGE: Who?

SAM: *(starts stroking MARGE's hair)* My horse. Bobby. *(strokes MARGE's uniform)* Brown. Big brown Bobby. I loved Bobby.

VAL: She's one of those horsey girls.

MARGE: What?

VAL: You know. Those girls. They turn twelve, fall in love with their horse and they never look back.

MARGE: Oh yeah.

SAM: You have Bobby's eyes.

MARGE: Gee. Thanks.

SAM: Once, Bobby and I went over a jump. It was...it was.... *(gives a shudder)* I've always wanted to have control over that moment.

MARGE: You're absolutely right. One mustn't let those moments escape.

VAL: You're humouring her?!

MARGE: I've always had a certain yen for bald women on roller skates.

> *SAM is fingering MARGE's uniform.*

VAL: But she's crazy!

MARGE: So, it'll be a fling.

VAL: I thought you were celibate.

MARGE: Celibacy is not what it's cracked up to be. *(to SAM)* Please, tell me more about Bobby.

SAM: We used to go to shows together.

VAL: Movies?!

MARGE: Horse shows. Really, Val, don't break the mood.

SAM: Bobby used to travel in a little van. He'd wear an orange blanket. I used to sleep next to him.

MARGE: I have a van.

SAM: You do? Where?

MARGE: Out front.

SAM: I want to see it. I want to see it NOW!

> *SAM skates flirtatiously out the front door. MARGE follows. She smiles and shrugs at VAL.*

MARGE: Tomorrow. We'll land another D.B. tomorrow. *(leaves)*

ANDREW: D.B.

VAL: *(smiles)* D.B.

ANDREW: Now say the whole thing. Slowly.

VAL: Delinquent Borrower.

> *ANDREW pulls VAL down onto the couch.*

Scene 7

The next day. VAL comes into the living room to find ANDREW packing his knapsack.

ANDREW: *(sees VAL)* Oh. Hi.

VAL: Going somewhere?

ANDREW: Well—ah—I had a huge crush on you.

VAL: Had?

ANDREW: I guess you knew that.

VAL: No.

ANDREW: Well—that's why I hung around.

VAL: You're talking in the past tense.

ANDREW: And I could always pass it off by saying it was just my fetish but—ah—it's very real right now.

VAL: Yes! *(kisses him)*

ANDREW: *(pulls away)* It's great. I mean, really great. I can't deal with it.

VAL: What?

ANDREW: It's too good. I'm too attracted to you. That's wrong. I shouldn't be that attracted to someone.

VAL: What?

ANDREW: Maybe if we didn't have sex. I could stay, then.

VAL: No, no. No, don't do this to me.

ANDREW: I mean, do you just want me as an affair?

VAL: Yes!

ANDREW: I can't do that. I don't want to lie to Cyril.

VAL: Okay, we'll tell him.

ANDREW: I don't want to be part of a triangle.

VAL: Okay, I'll leave him.

ANDREW: This is serious, Val. You two should work it out.

VAL: Work what out!

ANDREW: I have to go. It's the right thing to do.

VAL: No!!

ANDREW: I don't want to break up your marriage. This might just be some weird sexual thing.

VAL: It is! It is! STAY!!!

ANDREW: This is for the best. *(leaves)*

> *VAL collapses on the front door step. MARGE walks in.*

MARGE: *(cheerful)* Well, let's go bust some heads!

> *SAM wanders by. She holds her shaver and listens to it.*

MARGE: *(to SAM)* Hi, babe. *(slaps her bum)*

SAM: Who the fuck are you? *(exits)*

MARGE: Someone got out of the wrong side of the van this morning. What's going on?

VAL: She doesn't recognize you.

MARGE: I'm her horse.

VAL: Yesterday, you were her horse. Today, you're a total stranger. Yesterday, I was in love. Today, I'm abandoned. *(gazes out the door)*

MARGE: Oh. *(pause)* I thought we'd nail the U. of T. professor.

VAL: *(distracted)* He's my husband's twin brother.

MARGE: No kidding?

VAL: I was thinking of inviting him for dinner. *(laughs maniacally)*

MARGE: Good. That'll distract him while I put the cuffs on him. *(drags VAL out)*

Scene 8

Basement of CYRIL X's home. VAL and MARGE whisper in the darkness. MARGE has a small flashlight.

MARGE: Phooooouuuueeeee! What a stink!

VAL: Why are we prowling around in his basement?! Why don't we just knock on his door and talk to him?

MARGE: He didn't talk to you the last time.

VAL: Yes, but now, I'm family.

MARGE: And even better reason for keeping the door locked.

VAL: Oooooooouuu. *(talks through her nose)* What do you think that smell is?

MARGE: I dunno. A dead rat. The smell of literature deconstructing?

VAL: Aaah! I just bumped into something.

MARGE: Books?

VAL: No. It's soft and aaaah! It's a body!!

MARGE: No wonder it smells in here. There's a rotting composting body in the basement.

VAL: Oh God! He's a serial killer!

MARGE: I don't think so.

VAL: Why not?

MARGE: Doesn't fit the Personality Profile. Nah. Professors
aren't serialists. They're one shot guys. Axe murder.
Bludgeoning. That sort of thing. One-on-ones. Usually
with the wife. But maybe in this case, the Brother. Yes.
I'd say it's fratricide and Cyril's a Cyril killer.

VAL: *(disgusted)* Oh Marge.

MARGE: We should go look and see.

VAL: See what?

MARGE: See which one it is.

VAL: They're twins, Marge.

MARGE: Oh. *(pause)* Come on, let's look.

MARGE pushes VAL ahead of her.

VAL: Stop pushing! Marge!! Aaagh! Stop. We're here.

MARGE: *(shines flashlight down)* Yeah. That's a body all
right.

They both look.

VAL: It's not Cyril.

MARGE: It appears to be a total stranger.

VAL: Oh God, let's get out of here.

*MARGE and VAL head for the window. An overhead light
goes on. CYRIL X appears. He points a gun at them.*

111

CYRIL X: Not so fast!

MARGE: I am the Metropolitan—

CYRIL X: Sit down!

> *He shoves MARGE into a nearby chair.*

CYRIL X: Both of you!

> *VAL sits in a chair beside MARGE. CYRIL ties their hands behind their backs.*

CYRIL X: Awful smell.

VAL: I don't smell anything, do you, Marge?

MARGE: No. Not a thing.

> *MARGE and VAL laugh uneasily.*

CYRIL X: It smells of...putrefaction. Yes. The bubbling ferment of decomposing flesh. You must smell it.

VAL & MARGE: Not us! No, not us! Not a thing!

CYRIL X: Really? You know what that means.

VAL: You'll let us go?

CYRIL X: No. No sex drive.

VAL: What!

CYRIL X: Lack of olfactory sense. Affects the sex drive. Doesn't get triggered. No one home. Sexually, that is. It's odd that both of you would lack a sex drive.

MARGE: You're a fine one to talk, Buddy.

VAL: *(hisses)* Marge!

CYRIL X: I have an overwhelming sex drive.

MARGE: Oh yeah, right. Listen Buddy, I've talked to your wife and you're awful.

CYRIL X: My wife is dead.

MARGE: How would you know. Lie still and take it. That's what we're all trained to do—

VAL: *(warningly)* Ma-a-arge! *(to CYRIL X)* Look, I just wanted to talk to you.

CYRIL X: And breaking into my basement seemed the best way of going about it?

VAL: I'm your sister-in-law.

CYRIL X: Weren't you here a few days ago, claiming to be my wife?

VAL: Yes—but—

CYRIL X: Is there a reason you're so determined to be a member of my family?

MARGE: Yeah, why, Val? They're all nuts.

VAL: *(ignores MARGE)* I'm married to your brother, Cyril.

CYRIL X: Oh. Him. There's really nothing to say. I hardly know the man. My parents put me in foster care when I was ten years old.

VAL: Why?

CYRIL X: Because I was Evil.

VAL: Oh, well—

MARGE: Nice surprise for your foster parents.

CYRIL X: I've always been remarkably well-adjusted. It's the people around me who suffer. *(pulls out a knife)* I think a knife is best, don't you? Guns are so obvious.

VAL: You're not going to kill us?!

CYRIL X: Yes I am, actually.

VAL: But you can't!

CYRIL X: I'm sorry, ladies but I'm a raging psychopath. I have a knife and we're in the basement. And you know what they say. LOCATION LOCATION LOCATION!

MARGE: You're a real-estate agent?

CYRIL X: *(shrugs)* Part-time.

MARGE: He really is evil, Val.

VAL: You're not evil!

CYRIL X: Oh, but I am. You see, there is the Good Twin and there is the Evil Twin. When the egg splits in two, there is a battle for survival. One embryo must dominate. Someone has to get in there first, as they say. And that twin gets more nourishment. His brain is bigger and better developed than his sickly brother's. Mind you, how nice can he be? His first instinct before he even has a brain is to push his embryonic sibling out of the way. But everyone calls him the Good Twin. Smug little bastard. Now the Evil Twin is left to rot. He doesn't get the nourishment he deserves. His brain is denied its proper supply of oxygen so he's stunted. He's not broad-minded and cheerful. He's narrow-minded and bitter. He obsesses. He schemes. He has Learning Disabilities. And when the two twins set off into the world, everybody LOOOOOVES the Good Twin. They can pick him out easily. He looks like a cherub. Ruddy cheeks and a ready smile. The Evil Twin looks identical, but not so pleasant. He is not smiling. He waits and bides his time.

VAL: Bides his time for what?

CYRIL X: Revenge.

VAL: Oh. *(pause)* Why?

CYRIL X: *(shrieks)* For stealing the placenta juices!!

MARGE: Ooh, yeah, that's pretty terrible. This doesn't look good, Val.

VAL: I know, Marge.

CYRIL X: *(suddenly looks at VAL)* You look a bit like my wife. Except, she was beautiful. That overwhelmingly putrid odour which neither of you smell is her decomposing body. I have these blackouts and then I don't remember. I must have gotten mad at her and done something.... Evil. So you see, Detectives, you've found me out and now you must pay!

MARGE: We're not detectives.

CYRIL X: You're not?

MARGE: No. I am the Metropolitan Public Library Book Collector and this is my assistant. We came for the deconstructivist literature.

CYRIL X: Oh that trash. It's in those boxes over there.

MARGE: Well, that's great. If you'll just untie us, then we'll pick up the books and be on our way.

CYRIL X: There's still the problem of my wife.

VAL: She's a problem. Yes. But that's not her.

CYRIL X: It's not? Well, who the hell is it, then?

VAL: I don't know. Some guy.

CYRIL X: Well, I don't think I would kill just some guy. Even in a psychopathic rage, I would think I'd be more particular than that. Oh God, so many distractions. Now where was I? Oh yes. *(pulls VAL's head back, is about to slit her throat)*

A buzzing sound is heard. CYRIL X stops.

OFFSTAGE VOICE: *(pronounced English accent)* Lyle?

CYRIL X: Samantha?

> *The buzzing gets louder as SAM comes down the stairs. She carries the electric razor. She is dressed in English riding gear.*

SAM: D-A-A-R-L-I-N-G!

> *CYRIL rushes over to her. They embrace and kiss and make little buzzing sounds with the razor till they reach a crescendo. Then they shut the razor off and sigh as if they'd experienced an orgasm. CYRIL X offers Sam a cigarette. MARGE and VAL look baffled.*

SAM: I thought you were dead.

CYRIL X: What a coincidence, darling. I thought you were dead.

SAM: Oh no, darling, I'm alive!

CYRIL X: I'm alive, too, darling. We're both alive!! Happy, darling?

SAM: Oh, more than you'll ever know!

MARGE: *(to VAL)* Christ, we're in trouble. They're both evil psychopaths.

SAM: Darling, who are those dreadful-smelling people and why are they tied up?

CYRIL X: Oh—ah—

SAM: Untie them, dear.

CYRIL unties VAL and MARGE.

SAM: You didn't go psychotic again, did you, sweetums?

CYRIL X: *(sheepishly)* Uh huh.

SAM: Well, I hope you didn't kill anyone. *(to VAL and MARGE)* He gets so lonely when I'm away.

VAL: There's a body over there.

SAM: What a nuisance.

> *CYRIL X, SAMANTHA, VAL and MARGE walk over to the body.*

SAM: Do you know him, darling? Was he one of your colleagues? *(to VAL and MARGE)* They're so vicious in Academia.

CYRIL X: *(muses)* There was that overly ambitious graduate student.

> *The body moves and groans. SAM, CYRIL X, MARGE and VAL shriek and leap back several feet in unison.*

BODY: Christ! Bad enough to be stranded in this godforsaken place. Bad enough to have no money for booze. But to be up and told you smell like one of the dead, well, if that ain't adding insult to injury. *(starts fondling CYRIL X)* You don't even recognize me, do you, boy?

CYRIL X: Father?

BODY: No. It's your Uncle Calvin.

SAM: Uncle Calvin! Aaaah! *(faints in CYRIL's arms)*

CYRIL X: Oh no, I've lost her! Samantha! *(pats her face to revive her)* Bloody hell, Uncle Calvin! You know she hates you.

CALVIN: It's so hard to keep track. They all look the same to me.

SAM: *(comes to as "SONDRA")* Hi, Lyle!

CYRIL X: Ooh, she's gone! My beloved's gone!

SONDRA: *(sniffs the air, turns and sees UNCLE CALVIN)* You need a bath, Uncle Calvin.

CALVIN: Don't rush me. How 'bout a kiss for your old uncle?

SONDRA shoves him away and goes to see CYRIL X who is crouched in a foetal position and sobs softly to himself.

CALVIN: Geez! Sorry I asked.

CYRIL X: Samantha. The light of my life.

SONDRA: He's so serious when he's Lyle.

VAL: You mean Cyril and Lyle are—

SONDRA: Cyril and I are married. And Lyle and Samantha are married. Same people. Married twice.

VAL: You both have split personalities?

SONDRA: Yup. He's got two. I've got three. He's developing a third one.

VAL: *(sobbing with rage)* Then who the fuck's Andrea?!

SONDRA: Andrea?

VAL: Andrea! The dental hygienist! The NICE SISTER!!!

CALVIN: Ooooh! Please. Don't shout. My head.

SONDRA: She doesn't exist.

VAL: *(spitting the words out)* I am really glad that one of you doesn't exist! Is this incest! Are you two brother and sister?

SONDRA: We don't like to call it incest. We like to use another term—

VAL: No! Don't tell me! You're evil. The two of you are just plain evil.

SONDRA: No, really, we're not evil. We're victims of our environment. We're not responsible.

VAL: *(goes over to CYRIL who is still curled up and sobbing)* *(speaks softly)* Cyril? Oh C-y-y-r-i-l. It's safe. You can come out now. Come on out, Cyril.

CYRIL: *(stops sobbing, looks up at VAL)* Val?

VAL: Cyril, is that you?

CYRIL: Yes.

VAL: Good. *(kicks and pummels him)* YOU PRICK! YOU SHITHEAD!!

CYRIL: OW!

VAL: Dye my hair! Get new glasses! Shave my head! Be nice to that fucking sister! Tie me up and try and slit my throat! And we weren't even married!! I'LL KILL YOU!! *(kicks him)*

CYRIL: Ooof! It's good to get the anger out of your system. OW!

VAL: I mean it, Cyril. I'm gonna kill you!! RIGHT NOW!! *(grabs a pillow and tries to smother him)* ONE PERSONALITY AT A TIME!

> *MARGE and SONDRA rush over and haul VAL off CYRIL.*

CYRIL: *(gasping, to SONDRA)* Boy, she was mad!

SONDRA: I know, darling. Other people simply don't understand. I'm the only woman for you. You know that now, don't you.

CYRIL: Yes, Sondra.

> *SONDRA helps CYRIL get up. The two of them clasp each other around the waist and walk out.*

SONDRA: I love you, Cyril.

CYRIL: I love you too, Sondra.

MARGE: You okay, Val?

> *VAL nods.*

MARGE: You're well rid of him.

VAL: Them.

MARGE: Well, look on the bright side. You didn't marry a murdering psychopath.

VAL: I've never been married. All this time and we weren't even married.

MARGE: *(looks around)* It's not a dead loss.

VAL: It's not?

MARGE: We still have the books.

VAL: The books, the books....

MARGE goes to take the books.

CALVIN: *(lunges at box and clings onto it)* PLEASE NO! NOT THE BOOKS

MARGE: You stole them?

CALVIN flings himself onto MARGE's leg.

CALVIN: Yes. I'm the book thief. Punish me! *(looks up at MARGE)* You've got lovely thighs.

MARGE: *(kicks him off her leg)* Pervert!

CALVIN: Good God! What was I thinking! You're not Family!

MARGE: These books are the property of METRO!! *(grabs box away from CALVIN)*

CALVIN: Please! No! Please! Just leave me with one small book!

MARGE: NO! *(smiles)* God's in His Heaven. All's right with the world.

> *MARGE looks at VAL to join her. VAL motions for her to leave her alone for a while. MARGE exits with the books. UNCLE CALVIN staggers after her.*

Scene 9

Basement of CYRIL X's home. Some time later.

VAL: Now, let me understand this correctly. You'd like a book on the Seasons. No. There's no book on "The Seasons." Not in this branch. There's no book. YOU JUST HAVE ME. *(announces)* THE SEASONS. There are FOUR seasons. Spring, Summer, Fall and Winter. Sound familiar? Good. SPRING. "April showers bring May flowers." "Spring is sprung. The grass is riss. I wonder where the birdies is." Okay—everything grows in the Spring. Plants, flowers, birds, puppies—all that stuff. Got it? Good. SUMMER. Things are still growing. Getting bigger. Fruit happens. You eat it. Got it? Good. FALL. Everything turns from green to red and brown. The leaves change colour and fall off. Hence—Fall. WINTER. It gets really cold. All the time. And everything DIES!

MARGE has brought ANDREW to the basement door. They peer in at VAL who now sits in a stupor. ANDREW hesitates. MARGE hands him a book. ANDREW enters.

ANDREW: Hi.

VAL ignores him.

ANDREW: I have a book outstanding.

VAL: No. No, you returned all your books.

ANDREW: You think I returned all the books but there was this one book which you forgot about. It's a very special book. A complex book. Mind you, its author is eccentric so the first chapter was somewhat cantankerous.

VAL: And the second chapter?

ANDREW: The second chapter showed promise but it was the third chapter that hooked me. I haven't been able to put it down. But then, I realized that I couldn't keep the book to myself. So, I've come back to ask you to please renew it. *(holds the book out to VAL)*

VAL: Is this a happy book?

ANDREW: It could be. I haven't finished reading it.

VAL: How many chapters does this book have?

ANDREW: As many as you like.

VAL: *(takes ANDREW's hand and stamps it)* Renewed!

THE END

PRODUCTION NOTES

Both productions of this play were done on very small narrow stages. If you must do it in a small space, do not use any furniture. Each time, the action stops to accommodate the removal and shifting of furniture, the comedy dies. The only way to avoid this, is to perform the play on a stage wide enough to accommodate different scenes so you can move the action from one area to another. It is important that there should be no blackouts between scenes unless specified in the script.

WIGS

You need two short blonde crew-cut style wigs for Val and Sam, one long dark-haired wig for Val, a long blonde-haired wig for Sondra and a long-haired wig for Andrew Blett.

IN AN IDEAL WORLD

The actress playing Sam will shave her head. It doesn't have to be a shaved bald head. It can be a G.I. pig-shave. That actress will wear two wigs: one long-haired blonde wig for Sondra, and a crew-cut style wig for Sam (Act One, Scene 13).

The actress playing Val will be willing to cut her hair short and dye it blonde. In which case, you need only one dark-haired wig.

THE BALD THING

If the actress is not willing to shave her head, this is how much work is involved if one wants to "fake" it. I should mention that in a small space, the bald cap does not look like a bald head. It looks like a bathing cap. In a larger space with more distance between the actors and audience, the bald cap would be very effective.

It takes an actress one and a half hours to apply the bald cap. With practice, the time can go down to 45 minutes. The bald caps and makeup are very expensive. I suggest contacting a make-up person in film. Bald heads come under the category of make-up, not wigs. A bald cap lasts for 2 shows (maximum 3).

You need an experienced "bald make-up" person to teach the actress and her bald-pate assistant to apply the bald cap each night.

It's easier if the actress has short hair. You wet the hair, slick it back and then you put spirit gum all over the head.

A special bald cap has to be cut. The tricky part is cutting it correctly. In the Toronto production, the make-up artist left the demonstration model on a wig stand so they could use it as a guide to cutting the others.

The cap is glued down around the edges of the skull. Then you need special make-up which is also very expensive. Most important, you need a VERY SKILLED apprentice to apply it correctly each night so that it looks real.

THE BLONDE THING

This is another option, which I used in desperation because we didn't have access to the right wigs. You forego the bald thing entirely. You make it about being "blonde."

To do this, the actress playing Val must be willing to dye her hair blonde. She doesn't have to cut it, but she must dye it blonde. The actress playing Sondra/Sam must be willing to cut her hair very short and dye it fake blonde.

You outfit Val with a dark brown long-haired wig for the first scenes of the play. You outfit Sondra with a long, lion's mane blonde-haired wig. Line changes to do "The Blonde Thing":

Act One, Scene 6, page 29

CYRIL: Oh, I shouldn't have said that. No, no, of course, I desire you. Just not now. Sometime, I'm sure it will all come flooding back. Maybe if you dyed your hair blonde.

VAL: Dye my hair blonde?

CYRIL: You'd look sexy with blonde hair. Lemon blonde!

VAL: Fake blonde....etc.

Act One, Scene 8, page 35

SONDRA: Bury the past, eh.

VAL: Yes.

SONDRA: Why did you dye your hair blonde?

Act One, Scene 13, page 66

SAM: A new start!

She raises the shaver in the air.

Act Two, Scene 6, page 105

MARGE: I've always had a certain yen for blonde women on roller skates.

Act Two, Scene 8, page 121

VAL: Dye my hair! Change my clothes! Get new glasses! Be nice to that fucking sister...etc.